The Other Marconi

Eugenio Michael Albano

authorHOUSE®

AuthorHouse™
1663 Liberty Drive
Bloomington, IN 47403
www.authorhouse.com
Phone: 1 (800) 839-8640

This book is a work of non-fiction. Unless otherwise noted, the author and the publisher make no explicit guarantees as to the accuracy of the information contained in this book and in some cases, names of people and places have been altered to protect their privacy.

© 2016 Eugenio Michael Albano. All rights reserved.

No part of this book may be reproduced, stored in a retrieval system, or transmitted by any means without the written permission of the author.

Published by AuthorHouse 11/05/2016

ISBN: 978-1-5246-4331-7 (sc)
ISBN: 978-1-5246-4333-1 (hc)
ISBN: 978-1-5246-4332-4 (e)

Library of Congress Control Number: 2016918574

Print information available on the last page.

Any people depicted in stock imagery provided by Thinkstock are models, and such images are being used for illustrative purposes only.
Certain stock imagery © Thinkstock.

This book is printed on acid-free paper.

Because of the dynamic nature of the Internet, any web addresses or links contained in this book may have changed since publication and may no longer be valid. The views expressed in this work are solely those of the author and do not necessarily reflect the views of the publisher, and the publisher hereby disclaims any responsibility for them.

Contents

Introduction vii
Chapter 1: The Early Years 1
Chapter 2: A Simple Love Story 4
Chapter 3: The Black Hand 7
Chapter 4: Growing Up in Calabria 10
Chapter 5: The Chicken Thief… 13
Chapter 6: Final Years in Calabria 16
Chapter 7: Coming to America 20
Chapter 8: Ellis Island and the Name Change............22
Chapter 9: Assimilating in the New World.................24
Chapter 10: Michele meets his Father...........................27
Chapter 11: Filling in the Blanks 33
Chapter 12: A First Crush 37
Chapter 13: A Marriage takes place..............................42
Chapter 14: A Chain of Events 46
Chapter 15: The Audition 51
Chapter 16: The Waiting Game 58
Chapter 17: Elizabeth's Revenge...................................65
Chapter 18: A Marriage in Progress..............................69
Chapter 19: A Time for Celebration 71
Chapter 20: The Families Grow But Not Before Tragedy Strikes....77
Chapter 21: Tragedy Comes in Threes 81
Chapter 22: Good News Follows and New Additions.....................85
Chapter 23: In Common with Eddie Cantor.................88

Chapter 24:	The Naked Lady	92
Chapter 25:	A New title for the Misses	96
Chapter 26:	Marconi	98
Chapter 27:	Naughty Marconi	102
Chapter 28:	An Unexpected Arrival	105
Chapter 29:	Distance…and the Hearts Grow Fonder	109
Chapter 30:	New Friends, New Interests	111
Chapter 31:	Independence Day	114
Chapter 32:	Farewell to Mrs. Prudential	118
Chapter 33:	New Roles - New Identities	119
Chapter 34:	Monopoly Played Once Again	122
Chapter 35:	Compassion Has Its Price	127
Chapter 36:	Becoming of Age---Asking the Question	131
Chapter 37:	And the Band Plays On	134
Chapter 38:	Retirement	138
Chapter 39:	Play it Again Sam!	142
Chapter 40:	Happy Days are here Again	144
Chapter 41:	The Winter of Their Lives	146
Dedication		151
Acknowledgment		153

Introduction

When I was a boy of eight or nine, my father began sharing stories with me of his youth in Calabria, Italy in the region known as Reggio-Calabria and more specifically, his small olive-rich village of Oppido Mamertina.

Unfortunately, I was not very interested in those stories then; they seemed so far off in both time and geographical proximity from my hometown of Philipsburg, Pennsylvania.

Years later, as a mature adult, I regretted that I hadn't made time for those stories because I realized how important they must have been to my father to share with me and now, in my later life, I realize how much that history and geographical knowledge would have benefitted me in the writing of this story. Even as a young adult, I was not aware that one day I would want to write his story and would be struggling to recover much of that information.

I am grateful to my sister, Joan, for having the wisdom to encourage my father to write a journal before his Parkinson's made it impossible for him to control a pen. Eventually, even though he might have been able to dictate that information, his illness would steal from him the mind that once was strong with recollection and rich in wonderful stories of the past.

It was that journal and a small black book, unknown to the family and to me…until just days before his passing that revealed that this Italian gentleman with Old World tradition and modesty, had kept a diary that no one would have suspected—a diary that

The Other Marconi

one might have thought would only be kept by a more worldly and modern American man.

It was a shared secret that made me realize just how much trust and confidence he had placed in me as his eldest son. It also allowed me to realize just how modern his thinking was.

So this story is about an Italian gentleman who had no shoes as a child because his family was so poor. As a matter of fact, most families in his village were no better off. And it's a story of his success as a father, a husband and the contribution he made to many other immigrant families with whom he had come to know as their insurance agent in the small hamlets that surrounded the counties of Clearfield and Centre Counties, where those immigrants lived and worked the coal mines of Central Pennsylvania.

My story will also tell of his transition into the New World and his success assimilating in the melting pot of modern America. However, that transition never caused him to forget his roots and his love for his native Italia. He valued his past to the extent of keeping a diary so that it could someday be shared by his son and those who might be privy to its contents.

Perhaps I will have some dates and timelines slightly out of sequence, but I will try to do justice to the man who became known to his wife and close friends as "The Other Marconi."

Chapter 1
The Early Years

My father told me that he hardly knew his father until he was nine years old. That seemed strange for an Italian family who would later be so close to one another and so dependent on the sons to provide for the family. But it was not unusual at the turn of the 19th century for poor Europeans to go wherever they could find work and later send for their families…especially when so many were trying to come to the New World.

Dominic Albano did not originally plan to leave his family for so long. His first departure from his village of Oppido Mamertina was traveling to Mexico to work as a laborer for a share-cropper who paid little more than survival pay. But even if it was little more than survival, it was an opportunity to have some employment that could lead to a better life for his family. However, when a dreadful epidemic reached Mexico, survival was defined as leaving before being shipped home in a wooden box!

The Spanish Influenza would not be labeled as such until the following decade, but tuberculosis, typhus, and cholera were all being experienced—and mostly among the foreign workers where living conditions were usually absent of any reasonable sanitary conditions, so it was not difficult to become vulnerable to those diseases.

Whatever the correct diagnosis would have been for the disease that swept over much of Mexico at the start of the 20th Century, it

The Other Marconi

was killing individuals like flies and gave reason for many of the surviving Europeans to return to their homes.

According to his journal, Michele (*pronounced Micale*) was only two when his father left for Mexico; the year was 1900. It was the following year that he left Mexico on the advice of a physician who was employed by the landowner and saw firsthand how the epidemic was claiming the lives of so many of the workers. He advised Dominic to return to his family, but instead he went directly to Naples where he was sure he would find work in the factories.

Michele would still not see his father for several years because there was not enough money for his father to send for the family. His father did send what he could each month to his family in Oppido, while his plan was to leave Italy after a short time to fulfill his dream for him and his wife and two sons.

As I recall, from his journal, there was one time when Dominic managed to send for his wife to join him for a few days in Naples before he left for the New World. Michele remembered his mother returning from that trip and telling her sons about their father and how he loved them so much.

I cannot be certain at what time within those early years in Italy that my father's mother relayed a rather personal and touching story to her sons—I would assume that it may have been closer to the time of their departure from Calabria—but it is a story worth telling at this point in time because it will establish the very beginning of this young family and the events that led to their very existence. While it is not unique to the formation of families at that time, the circumstances reveal the result of unusual fate.

And so I will interrupt the story of my father's youth in order to interject a story that was, years later, shared with me by my father. It is a story of timing and sheer coincidence that resulted in the marriage of my grandparents. And it explains the relationship of Michele to his brother Rocco.

As a teenage boy, the story did not mean so much to me, but now that I am able to appreciate its importance in the history of my family it means a great deal to me.

Chapter 2

A Simple Love Story

The story that was relayed to my father as a boy explains why he grew up with Rocco being his older brother, although he had been his father's first born son.

Elizabeth Trippodi had been married to Rocco Scolari, a barber, a tailor, and a musician, before she married my grandfather. My father told me this amusing and simple love story which allowed me to understand that not all marriages at that time in our history had been 'arranged marriages.'

Dominic and Elizabeth had grown up as best friends in the poverty-stricken area of Calabria. Rocco Scolari was a third cousin of Dominic's and married Elizabeth. But Dominic had not been invited to their wedding. There was no real explanation, but he did not attend.

As the story goes…one day when Dominic went to Rocco for a haircut, he saw Elizabeth there and made the remark that he was disappointed that he had not been invited to their wedding. Elizabeth explained that Rocco was in charge of the invitations and not her. Dominic responded by telling her that in that case, when he married he would invite her to his wedding, to have the first piece of wedding cake, but not Rocco. The statement was made in jest, rather than containing any real bitterness against his cousin.

The Scolari wedding must have taken place early in the 1890's because a year after the marriage a son was born to the couple;

his name was Stefano. At birth the child was diagnosed as having serious health complications and he did not survive beyond the age of one.

It was almost a year later, in 1895 that Elizabeth became pregnant a second time and was experiencing a great deal of illness with the pregnancy. Rocco was usually by her side, but an event was approaching that required him to leave her in order to perform in the band in which he was a member. It was an important event.

Rocco hated to leave his pregnant wife, but kneeled by her side asking God to be with her during his absence. In his prayers, he also pleaded with God that if He needed to take one of them it should be him and not his wife.

Elizabeth told her son that there had been a terrible heat wave that hit southern Italy at that time. Rocco had accepted a very cold beverage while being overheated from a combination of the hot sun and his exertion from performing outdoors in the sweltering heat. The combination of the conflicting temperatures brought about a serious sun stroke that claimed his life within days of that engagement. It was some months later, in January of 1896 that she gave birth to a son who she named Rocco.

Shortly thereafter, Dominic and Elizabeth began seeing each other. And a year after Rocco Scolari's passing, Dominic proposed to Elizabeth and in the summer of 1897 the couple was married. So the promise came true; Elizabeth would be at the wedding and indeed would have the first piece of wedding cake. It's ironic how those forecasts can sometimes play out!

In June of the following year, Elizabeth gave birth to her third son, Michele. It was the name of Dominic's father and, as was the custom, the first son was given the name of the father's father. *When the child is a first daughter, the father's mother is honored in the same way.*

So Rocco and my father grew up as brothers and…very close brothers. Both Dominic and Elizabeth made certain that these two boys would never think of themselves in any other way except the sons of Dominic and Elizabeth Albano. It was Elizabeth who was most instrumental in keeping this relationship between her sons a very tight one since Dominic did not re-enter his family's lives until several years later.

Later in my life there would be many occasions when I would witness just how close these two brothers were. It was only at Ellis Island that the boys were separated by name, however, due to a sad mistake made by the person who processed my Uncle Roy's papers. But even that terrible mistake would never come between Rocco and his younger brother.

Chapter 3
The Black Hand

At the turn of the 19th century The New World was not only becoming home to a whole new crop of European immigrants who would continue staking claim to gainful employment much as the first Pilgrims had done earlier in our history, and in forging new communities that contributed to the 'melting pot,' but it attracted another set of immigrants from Italy and the island of Sicily: they were the crime families.

By 1903 New York City became home to one of those crime families who had been known in Italy as the *Ndrangheta,* a Mafia-type crime organization based in Calabria. It was the Piromalli clan who would migrate to America where they would influence construction and spread to other parts of the states becoming very powerful and influential in various pockets of business and politics.

In Calabria this crime organization had been known as *La Mano Nera* or **The Black Hand**. That was the only name that my father had ever relayed to me: The Black Hand or…as he would say, "The Black Handers!"

As a child, my father had known of this criminal organization and had learned to fear them. Their roots were very close to his home of Oppido Mamertina because a branch of that family had made its home in the neighboring town of Gioia Tauro.

Even today, that small Calabrian town has remained infamous due to the organized crime that finds its home there. Although my father never came in direct contact with this organization, their existence created a fear that remained with my father long after he became a citizen of the United States.

He admitted that while this crime organization was feared, it also protected the members of the Italian community in the region of Reggio Calabria. The poor citizens of that region looked up to the group as a type of government…it was their idea of a government-controlled state. They owned the heads of government and took money regularly as though it were an expected taxation on its citizens.

The unfortunate existence of this crime family was evident in the failure to enjoy freedom of speech—even years later when their presence ceased to maintain the strong political hold that it once had.

It was his mother who taught her sons to stay clear of their presence and never to say a bad word about them. The mention of their name, "La Mano Nera" was always spoken in a whisper. And whatever that organization stated was set down as law.

There were many times during my teen age years that my father would advise me to stay quiet about political opinion or other ideas that might be socially controversial. It was often difficult for me to convince my father that I was exercising a right that I enjoyed as an American citizen. And I did enjoy making my opinions known…sometimes in friendly discussions and later in newspaper commentary. Nevertheless, he feared reprisal from those whom I may have offended.

And so Michele and Rocco grew up knowing this fear of The Black Hand. That fear will become obvious in the following chapter when stealing from *la famiglia* was not tolerated… especially when it was done by another family.

Author's note

The influence of organized crime still exists and is reflected by the presence of certain crime families in the most southern region of Italy and…as is stated below, within the very town where my father was born. Their method of justice will be shown in a following chapter where that organization has its own menu for just punishment among its people.

A high-profile case occurred as recent as July 2014, when a procession in Oppido Mamertina made a detour and performed a "salute" beneath a flat where Giuseppe Mazzagatti, 82, a convicted mob boss, was serving a life sentence under house arrest. He was not in prison because of his advanced age. The gesture was all the more awkward for the Vatican because it came a month after Pope Francis visited Calabria – the heartland of the powerful 'Ndrangheta mafia – and launched a scathing attack on organized crime, announcing that all mafiosi were excommunicated from the Church, condemning them to hell in the afterlife. (Google)

Chapter 4
Growing Up in Calabria

'The Boy without Shoes'

My father did not recall much from his earliest years as a child in Oppido Mamertina, but he did remember that they were very poor. He never did know if his parents rented the house that they lived in or had built it on rented ground. There were very few landowners in his village; a few prominent families owned most of the ground and allowed the villagers to build their simple structures on that ground.

The ground level of his family home was just that…walls built on the ground as its foundation. There was no sub-floor or solid structure; it was just a frame built on the raw ground. But it was not a problem in that part of Italy because it was almost always warm and the climate was steady.

That dirt floor of many homes was kept as shelter for the animals, while the family occupied the 'prima piano,' or the second floor, which in most European cultures is considered the first floor.

My father told me that the living quarters (built above the ground floor for their animals) consisted of two rooms: a cucina (or kitchen) and a large room that had a dividing partition to separate the parents sleeping quarters from the children's. He explained that there was no door; it was not a separate room, but the partition allowed a minimum degree of privacy for the parents.

Of course my father only remembers his mother occupying that section of the sleeping quarters. "We were proud to own a goat and some chickens," he told me. The goat supplied them with milk, while the chickens' eggs brought them a small income.

I also recalled learning that my father never had a pair of shoes until he was almost nine years old. He and his brother, Rocco, went barefoot most of the time. However, by the time he was five and Rocco was seven, his brother made them sandals out of some course material that came from the bark of the tree. *(There was another product that was made from the bark of a tree, and I'll come back to that)*.

Elizabeth did manage to have shoes made for both of her sons from a local shoemaker just months before they sailed to America in 1907.

When I questioned my father about living without shoes, he relayed a story that had been told to him by his father years later. Perhaps the story was told to him at a time when the conversation turned to those early years in Calabria. He began by saying, "I once thought I was poor because I had no shoes until I saw the man who had no feet! Then I knew that I was not poor." It was only one of many tales that explained my father's profound humility and gratitude for the life he had.

There was a great deal of bartering in his village of Oppido Mamertina. In fact, that was the method used in order for him and his brother to have shoes. In addition to selling their eggs, his mother also took in some washes…although, it was not really taking them in, but taking the wash down to the river along with some of the other women. "There was an elderly widower who lived near our house and also a woman who was sickly for a long period of time," he told me. "My mother took their clothes along with ours when she did the wash."

I believe that in order to have their shoes made, his mother did several months of sewing for the shoemaker. She explained that while he was clever at his craft, he did not have the knowledge or skill of sewing the small items of his clothing. And so my grandmother, whom I never knew, bartered for the shoes by doing wash and mending clothes for the shoemaker.

Chapter 5

The Chicken Thief…

One of the stories that my father told me as a young boy of ten or twelve was the one about the chicken thief. Perhaps he wanted to impress upon me the importance of honor among families and the high price one might pay for the crime of theft. I found a version of this story later when I found his diary.

Yes, my father was not always the typical old fashion, old world man that some would have expected him to be. He was a quiet man and very much a gentleman…a handsome gentleman, according to early photos. But he certainly would have never been figured to be one that kept a diary, and yet there was that little black book that contributed so much in making this story possible.

The incident occurred when my father was about eight and his brother would have been ten. It was just a year before he left his homeland to join his father in America. The story involved two families who lived in his village. The victim of the theft was Mrs. Fortino, a young widow who had lost her husband to a fishing accident in the Adriatic. She had young children and survived by also having chickens which she raised for their eggs and for consumption. "She was not in direct competition with our chickens," he told me, "because she lived on the other side of the village and had her own group of customers."

The other family in this story was that of Guido Costello, the middle son of a landowner, and a boy who couldn't seem to stay out of trouble. But his father's prominence in the community

The Other Marconi

usually allowed him to enjoy his mischief. It was rumored that Guido's father was connected to the crime families, but it was never proven.

Guido decided to take one of Mrs. Fortino's chickens one evening and told his friend—who was the wrong person to tell. The boy, to whom he admitted the theft, did not want to have any part of this crime…even being aware of it, so he relayed the story of theft to his mother.

Within a week of the missing chicken, Guido was said to have had a terrible accident that resulted in four of his fingers being cut to the knuckles. The news of Guido's severed fingers traveled from one end of the village to the other. News of such a terrible accident traveled almost as swiftly as the sharp instrument that would have caused such a horrible accident. It was said that he had caused the accident when he was using some sharp tools from his father's tool shed. But Guido was not known to do much work on his father's land.

The family owned acres of rich olive trees and they had common laborers from the village who harvested those rich olives. What instrument or tool could have brought about such a monstrous accident: the severing of the fingers of his right hand? Of course the boy was right-handed so it did explain the hand which resulted in the cruel dismemberment.

The truth became known after several days of whispers throughout the village. But only a few people dared to repeat what was being said about the boy's severed hand. Rocco was privy to the true story and relayed it to my father; there was very little that these brothers kept from one another! He told my father that the story told was only a cover-up to avoid a scandal within the Costello Family.

No one in the village was aware that Mrs. Fortino was a cousin of the Piromalli crime family who resided in Sicily. When her cousins learned of the theft, they weren't concerned about Guido's father's connections to another one of the families from Gioia Tauro. It was a shame within the 'families' for one family to steal from another and so the fingers were severed to teach the lesson. My father had to promise his brother that he would not tell their mother who had provided him with the real story.

Michele admitted that once he was told of the intentional removal of Guido's fingers, he figured that it was the just punishment for thievery. It was not until he came to America that he realized that corporal punishment was not the norm for a simple theft—at least not the removal of fingers for the theft of small property and certainly not by the law of the land!

It was the 'chicken thief' story that my father contributed to his deep respect for keeping his hands to himself. However, that is not entirely true, as we shall learn later when I share what had become an ongoing problem within the early years of my parents' marriage.

Chapter 6
Final Years in Calabria

Not every day in the small town of Oppido Mamertina was there much to talk about. And there was little time for idle discussion since there were chores to be done and little money to consider for the basic needs. Brother Rocco was charged with the chore of milking the goat because Michele's mother knew him to be the stronger boy and of course he was two years older than my father. Michele was in charge of keeping the chickens fed and in line if they gave the rooster any problem. They were there to keep the rooster happy and to produce eggs…lots of eggs!

My father assured me that he was not a weakling, although he was not as big and strong as his brother. He confirmed that by letting me know that he often carried the wash down to the river for his mother and carried wood for the cooking stove.

It was not often that warmth was needed by manufactured heat in his village since the region of Reggio was known to be seasonally warm and quite calm for sleeping. However, there were days when manufactured air conditioning would have been welcomed, but of course that luxury was not even known of at the time. And if it had been, it would not have reached the area of Calabria…not even for the few that would have been considered to be of the privileged class—and they were very few! It would have been scandalous to indulge in such luxury. Besides…it is doubtful if these small houses enjoyed electricity.

Even now, in modern times, it is not uncommon to find the wash being hung out on lines to dry. Many consider it an abuse of electric energy to own a clothes dryer, but perhaps a more reasonable explanation would be the prohibitive cost of having adequate electrical current brought in to replace old wiring.

Along with the usual chores was the constant responsibility of caring to be sure that you were not cutting your feet on fallen debris from trees or sharp stones that may be lying within the paths of the rough roads and trails. Medication for such cuts and accompanying dressings would have been too much of a luxury to require as a norm.

It was only after many cuts and bruises to the feet that brother Rocco began to create sandals for himself and my father. My father admitted that it was he who was the recipient of so many cuts from sharp stones on the dirt roads. He told me that he was grateful to his brother for so much attention to his personal needs such as the sandals that were made from pieces of leather strips that were gathered from the shoemaker's shop. Those scraps replaced the more primitive construction of sandals that Rocco had constructed from the bark of the tree.

And speaking of the bark from trees, let's go back to an earlier story that I was told…that in those days the only flour that was available for making bread was that which was made by producing a meal that was ground from the bark of trees. My father could not be certain if it were only the bark of certain trees or just any bark. But he did recall that it was from the bark that his mother was able to produce a farina or flour from which bread was made.

He told me that the bread was very hard to chew, but his mother assured him that he would have stronger teeth as a result of chewing the hardened chunks of bread. I suppose that the fiber count was quite exceptional…if one can imagine that being a benefit!

The Other Marconi

At the first reading of my father's papers, I thought that his father had remained in Naples for a longer period of time, but the journal states otherwise. So it was either 1902 or 1903 when Dominic Albano, with his cousin Joseph Federico, arrived in Clearfield, Pennsylvania where the Federico family would open a grocery store. It is uncertain what type of work was available for Dominic in Clearfield, but the following year he moved to Morrisdale where he began his employment in the coal mines. My father even detailed the fact that his father worked in mine shaft #1 of the Morrisdale Coal Company.

During those next three years, Elizabeth and her two sons continued living on very little in their village of Oppido (as I shall at times refer to that hamlet), with the promise that someday soon they would be sent for and would join Dominic in The New World.

Photo of Mineshaft #1
Photo Courtesy of The Philipsburg Historical Foundation

Chapter 7

Coming to America

The first opportunity to join Dominic came in 1906, when Dominic had saved enough money for his family to join him. He had been successful in renting a small house in Oak Grove, a settlement not far from Morrisdale. He shared that home with his brother, Francesco, who had subsequently come to America, and his cousin, Joseph Federico, who left Clearfield to also work in the mines. So the three men shared the rental of that small house in Oak Grove.

Dominic purchased tickets for his family to travel by ship to the United States, but in that same year Rocco had turned ten in January and his required fare was considered that of an adult. So the tickets that Dominic had sent his wife were no longer valid for the voyage and the trip was postponed. Other events occurred that year, according to my father's journal, that also made the travel impossible at the time. There were coal mine strikes, he wrote, that made it impossible to put aside any additional funds. His father told him that if a man was earning twenty dollars ($20) for a two-week period, it was considered good pay.

During that same year there was a terrible earthquake in that region of Calabria but they were spared any physical harm and held out hope for their future in the New World: America!

Finally, in 1907, the family would be reunited. Elizabeth and her sons were taken to Gioia Tauro by a U.S. postal carriage. It must have been a terrible mode of transportation…even for that short trip because my father writes that all three of them took sick during that short ride. He explained that their seats were benches within boxcars. It must have been like a small train, only drawn by horses rather than an engine. That sickness continued to plague them for most of their voyage as they crossed the Strait of Gibraltar.

In order to make the deal for the voyage, Michele and Rocco offered to work aboard the ship by cleaning and scrubbing the deck. They were also charged with keeping the toilets cleaned. When I read that part of his journal, I could only relate to that experience from having a similar assignment of duties aboard the USNS Buckner when I crossed the Atlantic as a young Army Private in 1961. I dare say, however, that conditions were somewhat more favorable those many years later.

In his journal, my father writes that his mother was dreadfully ill during their voyage…so much so that the ship's master told them that if their mother were to die aboard ship they would have to throw her body overboard. "The idea of losing our mother in this way was frightening," my father wrote. He and his brother did everything possible to make their mother comfortable and attend to her illness.

My father was nine at that time and his brother was eleven. But it seemed that at eleven his brother was so much more mature than him in taking responsibility. Rocco assured his brother that their mother was not going to die and that they would never allow such a primitive burial for her!

One can only imagine the anxiety that must have been felt during those early years in our history when the future was so uncertain and yet full of promise.

Chapter 8

Ellis Island and the Name Change

Between my father's arrival in the New World and the family's re-union with their father, I cannot be certain of the exact number of weeks or months that passed. However, there were arrangements for the family of three to stay with friends of a friend of Dominic's in New Jersey. But I am assuming that the processing at Ellis Island must have occurred upon their landing in New York Harbor. And it was during that processing that an impatient worker at the Island caused a major change that affected our families going forward.

Because a legal adoption had not taken place in Italy for Rocco Scolari, then born to Elizabeth Scolari, Rocco's papers were not the same as that of his brother…my father, Michele. The folks at Ellis Island were processing hundreds or…perhaps even thousands arriving each day.

When they came upon Elizabeth whose sons were Rocco Scolari and Michele Albano they didn't take the time to learn how this had occurred. So someone at processing must have decided that Alberto sounded close enough to Albano—thus Rocco was processed through as Rocco Alberto and subsequently took on the name Roy Alberto. At the same time, my father was processed through as Michael Albano and accepted the new spelling.

Dominic was very disturbed when he learned by letter from Elizabeth that their older son no longer held the name that he had been proud to give him in Italy. But the family had no financial means to take the necessary action that would have corrected the mistake by legal adoption. They were focusing their energy on making a life for themselves in the New World and earning enough for that new life. And so eventually two families would develop from one: the Albano family and the Alberto family.

It seemed that there was an immediate desire to Anglicize the names at Ellis Island. And so the name 'Michele' that appeared on my father's birth certificate was no longer acknowledged, but instead was spelled and pronounced as Michael on all future documents. However, my father did retain a copy of his Italian birth certificate. And it was from that document that I realized the name that was given to him, rather than the Anglicized version which we only knew.

I then realized that my mother had not made up the name that she often called out to him pronounced: Micale. *(However, it should be noted that she only used that pronunciation when she was calling attention to some error he had made or a warning that he could be in the dog house!)*

The time that followed in New Jersey was somewhat blurred. There were English classes during half of the day and work during the remainder. When it came to translation, Michael was helping his older brother, who became instantly fascinated by so many girls in his English classes.

At the age of nine, puberty had not yet found my father and so he wasn't able to have the same appreciation and/or distraction that plagued his older brother. So his attention was focused on learning English as well and as quickly as possible.

It was gratifying, my father told me, that there was finally one thing that he could do for his brother rather than his reliance on him. And it gave Rocco a new reason to look up to his little brother as the 'smart little brother.'

Chapter 9
Assimilating in the New World

The processing through Ellis Island had been challenging for Elizabeth and her sons but the immediate weeks following were not too difficult since Dominic had arranged for his family to stay with relatives of friends in New Jersey. He had informed his wife, even before leaving Calabria, that there would not be an immediate reunion of family after their arrival. Money was still being saved from his bi-weekly pay so that he could provide for his wife and sons once they were re-united.

The Faggiano family, whose roots originated in Naples, were cousins of one of the men who worked alongside Dominic in the mines. They had offered Elizabeth and the boys lodging with only services required as payment. Sara Faggiano found Elizabeth temporary work in the sewing factory where she was employed; that income provided the transient family with money for food. Michele and Rocco helped Franco Faggiano in his shoe repair shop and delivered groceries for a nearby grocery store that was owned by another cousin of the Faggianos.

Rocco seemed more suited for assisting in the shoe shop since he had already shown an interest in making the sandals for him and his brother. Michele was pleased to be the delivery boy since he was eager to meet new people and was able to improve his English while delivering the groceries. Apparently his attraction to foreign languages shined through early because he would return to the family at the end of the day speaking a few words in Polish and German. It was a mixed neighborhood…although most of the customers were also Italian immigrants.

This transition from Italy to the New World turned out to be a positive one. There were no displays of prejudice or rejection. Perhaps this was one of the benefits in having Dominic's family begin their assimilation in New Jersey.

The communities of Linden and Elizabeth New Jersey were two of the towns that had been instrumental in welcoming those who had come across the Atlantic. After all, they were bedroom communities to New York City and there the melting pot was flourishing.

It was not until their pilgrimage to Pennsylvania that they heard the words, "Dago," "WOP," and "Greaseball!" Even then it was not very offensive because during the initial callings of these words Michele and Rocco did not fully understand the meaning of the words.

My father first thought that they were complimentary nicknames, and by the time he realized what they referenced, his skin was tough enough to let them roll off his back. Besides, those calling out such unkind epithets were in the minority of the community of miners and common laborers. Most of that general community were also immigrants who had been victims of other unpleasant name-calling associated with their homeland: the Irish, the Polish, and the Swedes were those who had weathered a similar storm.

Little did Rocco realize at the time that those early friendships would someday become the gateway for him and his family to regain New Jersey as their 'home state.'

By the time Michele met his father in Morrisdale, Pennsylvania he was speaking complete sentences in English and some meaningful phrases within the Polish and Scandinavian languages. Of course he was still most comfortable when at home with his parents where only Italian was spoken and understood by all.

It was impossible to know that not only would this attraction to other languages help him in the coal mines, but would later be an asset in his career which required an absolute affinity for European languages and a positive communication with families who were struggling with the English language.

Chapter 10
Michele meets his Father

Every day seemed like a week and every week like months but finally the day came when Michele and his brother, along with their mother, was preparing to join Dominic in Pennsylvania.

It must have been a journey filled with excitement and anxiety when my father traveled by train from New Jersey to Morrisdale, Pennsylvania. He wrote that he recalled them passing many towns along the way. He wrote that they passed a town called Marysdale, but I believe that he was probably referring to Marysville, Pennsylvania.

My father wrote of a new experience on that train ride. One man on the train informed Elizabeth that he knew her husband and knew that he would be eagerly awaiting their arrival; he pulled out some fruit from a paper bag and handed it to my father and his brother.

My father tells an amusing story of him and his brother biting into the fruit and experiencing the extreme softness of it (it was a banana). The boys looked at each other and whispered, "He thinks we don't have teeth to chew!" They threw the bananas out the window when the man wasn't looking. They were not familiar with this fruit and thought that they were being insulted for being foreigners.

One must assume that at that time there was train service to the small town of Morrisdale because he wrote about leaving the train and boarding a trolley car; he was amazed that there were no horses pulling the trolley!

I can only imagine the emotions that were built up in these two young boys when they were finally going to be reunited with a father who had been absent from most of their early years.

When they finally arrived by this 'engine-powered wagon,' he recalled hearing words that seemed magical to his ears; he wrote that sentence in his journal: "Michele, I am your father." He witnessed his father looking up at him while he sat in the carriage that delivered them from the train.

My father chocked with some emotion when he had earlier relayed this scene to me. And later, when reading this same sentence in his journal, it gave me that same feeling of tenderness and love that was being experienced between a father and his nine-year-old son.

It is worth noting here that my paternal grandfather was an opposite from my maternal grandfather. Although I never knew either of them, the accountings from both of my parents suggest that. And a subsequent conversation with my older sisters who had met our grandparents substantiates that assumption. My grandfather Dominic was a soft spoken gentle man who did not hide his love for his children. His wife had experienced a hard life while living apart from him, but perhaps was, by nature, a less passionate individual in displaying her emotions.

You might say that in today's definition of roles, Elizabeth later became the "bad cop," while her husband continued being the "good cop!" However, the 'bad cop' role was apparently only played when she thought that her young sons might be vulnerable to flirtations of the American girls and later towards my mother! She was very proud and very protective of her sons.

Michele knew his father as being soft-spoken and compassionate. He was not a disciplinarian, but rather a teacher and counselor to his sons. He taught them the gentle ways of becoming a gentleman without ever speaking the word 'gentleman.' He taught them the value of being kind and considerate of others—perhaps to a greater degree than any finishing school could have achieved.

Elizabeth was more of the protector of her sons, and it was she who arranged for both of her sons to have private music lessons soon after they became a family again in Morrisdale. Yes, Morrisdale became a permanent residence where they settled after living for a short period of time in the Oak Grove house. (*A bit more will become known about those lessons.*)

It was the following year on March 31st that Elizabeth gave birth to a fourth child (second in her marriage to Dominic): a daughter who they named Mary. If the child had been born in Italy, there is little question that the name would have been Maria, but to my knowledge it was Mary.

It was during that same year of 1908 that my father tells of witnessing their first snow. He had not seen these cold soft white flakes in his homeland of Italia. The weather was never very cold in the winter months, but sometime became quite hot during a short period of summer. The idea of changing seasons and especially the thrill of sled riding fascinated them.

1908 was also the year, at age twelve that Rocco joined their father in the coal mines as a young laborer. There was no emphasis on the legal age for young boys to work as miners. However, it was usually understood that a parent would not allow his son to enter the mines before the age of twelve. And in most cases the son worked alongside his father at that early age.

By 1910, at age twelve, Michael also began working alongside his father and brother into the dark world of coal mining. But my father continued attending public school half a day until 1913. When he had completed his fifth year of public school it was time to work fulltime so that he could become a major contributor to the family's needs for a comfortable survival.

Within the three years following the birth of the first daughter, a second daughter was born to Michele's parents and her name was Rose. I remind my readers that within the family Michael was still only referred to by his birth name, Michele. During his early years he had surely seen his life pass from childhood to adolescence quickly. But he was not experiencing the transition of chemistry that was taunting his brother who was now fifteen.

Rocco, now becoming known to all as Roy, was focusing with one eye on his work and the other on the young girls who never failed to show both of these boys an enormous amount of attention. And at this same time, Elizabeth was keeping both eyes on her sons, wanting to protect them from the flirtatious ways of the American girls. She was not so concerned about the girls from Italian families because she knew that they were on a short leash because of the Italian customs held by their parents.

With both brothers working in the mines and still learning the English language, there was little time to allow the bodies of adolescent boys to respond to the attention that the girls would have so desired. And Elizabeth was becoming more and more protective of her 'boys-to-men' sons.

Although he waited until he reached the age of twelve to enter the mines, my father held various odd jobs which contributed to the family's income. He assured me that by the age of ten he was already strong enough to help out with labor in construction and unloaded fruit and vegetable crates for a local store.

It was during this time, shortly after moving into their new quarters in Morrisdale, that Elizabeth began taking in a few boarders: men who rented rooms in my grandparents' home. And it was during this time that a musical instructor, known to the community as Professor Amato, came into the Albanos' lives and became available as the music teacher to Roy and Michael.

Elizabeth worked out a bartering system that included having the professor's meals furnished to him in exchange for the music lessons; Roy took lessons on the horn (believed to be the cornet) and my father learned to play the slide trombone.

By the time that Roy was seventeen and my father was fifteen, there became a short period when the brothers found themselves seeking different activities in their limited spare time. Roy was very much into girls while my father was still navigating those waters slowly and carefully. But they hadn't ever strayed far from each other, and when Roy realized that his younger brother was feeling left out, he began to bring him into his activities of flirting.

He once told my father, "Hey little brother (*mio piccolo*), it won't be long before you will discover girls too." But Michael assured him that he had 'discovered girls' but didn't know how to act among them. "Well," his brother assured him, "just watch me and do the same."

When my father realized that his brother liked pinching the girls and they didn't object, he decided that perhaps it was an approved sport and began to follow. He told me that his brother made a joke of the past in Oppido by assuring him that no one was going to cut off his fingers for touching. "You just have to touch without taking!" his brother had told him. He admitted that he wasn't sure what that message meant, but he nodded and followed suit.

So the young Italian boy who had been warned against stealing had found a pleasure in something less dangerous: pinching! However, my father found great delight in not only pinching the buttocks but enjoyed pinching the bosoms! And that little game got him in trouble when he found it difficult to abstain as a married man!

Later in our story, the memories of the chicken theft in Oppido Mamertina, and the resulting punishment of doing so, will again become a reminder of the severe punishment that can follow bad behavior. That topic will be re-visited before Michael becomes a married man.

Chapter 11
Filling in the Blanks

There was a great deal that occurred during the years between their arrival from Calabria and the time when my father would leave the Morrisdale Coal Mines in 1923. Part of this has been revealed in the following chapters, but the bits and pieces that may have been left out will be addressed within this chapter. And…if there is repetition, I would ask the indulgence of my readers.

There were three daughters born to Dominic and Elizabeth Albano after the family was reunited. We now have some idea as to when these children became a part of the family. According to my father's journal, his eldest sister, Mary was born in 1908 and his youngest sister, Nancy, was born in 1913. After some discussion with my cousin, Patti, I have concluded that her mother (my father's sister Rose) was born between 1910 and 1911.

In a later chapter we will see how relevant to my father's personal story is the status of his family and their welfare—the fact that family stayed together and supported one another according to the ability and perhaps the seniority of those remaining at home.

Supporting one's self during that era in our history was difficult enough, but supporting an entire family was indeed a struggle and the result of pride and the work ethic that followed them from their European roots.

There is little information to ascertain exactly what jobs my father may have held before he entered the Morrisdale Coal Mines to work alongside his brother Roy. At first, I believed that my father had not entered the coal mines until 1915, but after carefully reading some of his notes, I realize that both he and his brother were only twelve years old when they joined that labor force.

One can assume that a foreigner who was learning the New World language and taking whatever manual labor jobs could be thrown his way had little time to look back with any remorse. There was an energy and enthusiasm about the idea of chasing one's dreams where new horizons could be found.

The journal reveals that Michele, now becoming known as Michael, began his music lessons sometime prior to 1915 when he would reach the age of seventeen on the 1st day of June. We have already been made aware of how those music lessons were paid for, for both he and his brother—Michael playing the slide trombone and his brother playing the cornet. However, that practice of bartering may show up again in a future chapter.

It is not certain when my father became interested in another genre of music, but by the time I was old enough to recall my father's interests, opera was always an important part of his passion for music. Unfortunately, he never had the luxury of attending an opera at any of the great opera houses of the world. (*Perhaps I have tried to make up for that deprivation*).

There will be further mention of my father's passion for opera in a later chapter.

During those same years, Dominic Albano had been injured twice in the mines and had to turn to another mode of employment to support his family.

My father wrote that his father began repairing shoes and during that same time opened a small grocery store in the front room of their rented house. And of course, it was the taking in of boarders that allowed for the music lessons and supplemental income for the family.

The three men who each rented…or shared a room, cooked their own meals, but had their laundry done by Elizabeth and paid $1.50 per week for their lodging and laundry.

I cannot be certain what the pay was for miners during that time, but my father had noted that during the first years when his father was working in the mines an income of $20-$30 paid every two weeks was considered 'big money!'

I will assume, from the journal that during the period from 1915-1920 most of the income that supported the family as a staple of income was earned by my father and his brother since very little income could be generated from repairing shoes, and the small grocery store showed little profit in those days.

Being a miner at that time did not ensure steady work of five or six days per week because there were coal strikes that occurred frequently in the early years of the 1900's. In fact, in 1906, it was a major strike that made it impossible for many of the workers to save enough money to send for their families to join them in the New World. Even years later, men had to depend on three or four days of work per week to survive financially. There was virtually no job security at that time.

During these same years there were many Italian immigrants leaving their homeland to establish their families in the New World…perhaps the majority coming from the poorest region, identified as Calabria. And many of these immigrants were first, second and third cousins of those who had arrived before them. When they arrived, they all identified as '*la famiglia.*' And whether they actually became the godparents for their cousins' children, many were referred to as *Gomadi* and *Gompadi*, (godmother and godfather). These titles were used to show respect for their elders and to instill that respect in the children of those families.

Michael and Roy became familiar with several of these families: the Catalanos, the Prestipinos, the Serrafinos, the Catarinos…and the list went on. There was probably not much effort being made to assimilate until the early 1920's.

Until that time, the Italians stayed close to one another; the Polish stayed close to the Polish, and the Germans remained close to their own. But as employment brought these splinters of Europeans together and then melded them with those of British ancestry, the assimilation was in full force.

It was the close association of the Albanos with the Catalanos and Catarinos that led to Michael being introduced to the DeFazio family.

Although formal education ceased for my father after 1913, working in the coal mines, taking seriously his music lessons, and helping the family to operate a home grocery store left little time for leisure or recreation.

During that time in history, even with some small luxury of leisure time, there was not much casual dating allowed within the Italian families. Italian boys were still expected, by their families, to marry Italian girls. And the Italian families did not approve of dating unless plans for marriage had already been established. Even then, it was not common practice for an Italian girl to be privately in the company of her future husband without other family members being present. Virginity was not preferred. It was demanded!

Chapter 12

A First Crush

There was little time for any extracurricular activity soon after the brothers once again banned together. A year later, and just a month after my father's sixteenth birthday, his father fell ill. It began with headaches and a diagnosis of high blood pressure. Dominic had gained a considerable amount of weight once his family joined him, and he had also suffered numerous injuries while working the mines.

Now the boys had two jobs: they worked the mines during the day and worked at the family store in the evenings. They became very concerned about their father's health and feared losing a father that they had just begun to know.

They had found common ground in their lengthy conversations about the mines and the many accidents that occurred in those black holes. They found that their father was constantly praying that God would keep his sons safe when they were underground.

Shortly after their father fell ill, their mother's health also began to fail. That illness became more prevalent shortly after giving birth to her third daughter (my Aunt Nancy).

Later it was discovered that a form of anemia that had been diagnosed in Elizabeth was passed on to the youngest daughter. *It has been said that a form of Mediterranean Anemia is prevalent among those who originated from the area of Europe that borders on the Mediterranean, but I cannot confirm or substantiate that claim.*

The Other Marconi

With both of their parents experiencing ill health, the boys were almost entirely running the store while working fulltime in the mines. They made it appear as though they were just helping their parents, but in fact, they were contributing a full time effort to keeping the store going.

In spite of the heavy work load, by the time my father reached his seventeenth birthday (Roy was almost twenty and dating), he developed a crush which may have been 'puppy love,' or his 'first love,' albeit a one-way affair of the heart.

The brothers had enjoyed a limited social life that did make time for 'pinching' and…other touching. Roy reminded his brother that touching was not stealing, and for the most part they did confine their Italian antics to the single girls. However, there was one particular girl that Michael would not pinch because she was too special. Her name was Rosina Catalano.

Rosina was the only daughter in a family of six. Yes, she had five brothers who could be very protective! Michael and Roy had never witnessed that protection being necessary, but they only had to assume that five Italian brothers were not going to let their sister's heart be broken or…her property damaged by wild pinching.

Rosina's brothers: Frank, John, Carlo, Tony and Toby were known to be very protective of their sister. *By this time most of the young men were using short names to fit into the American society.*

As previously mentioned, within the family Michele and Rocco were still known by their given Italian names, but when the boys were out among their friends they were almost entirely known as Mike and Roy—I say 'almost entirely' because the Italian friends and relatives still preferred addressing them by their original native-Italian names.

Roy had not yet met Nervina Rizzo, the girl he would eventually marry. And my father was stuck on the idea of getting to know Rosina, but that dream never materialized. Rosina was a very attractive girl and from her appearance there was no doubt that she was somewhere between her mid and late teens.

None of the young men got very far in getting to know Rosina, however. Her father made it known that there was a man from Naples that would become her suitor upon his arrival from the Old Country. Apparently this man was the son of close friends of the Catalanos and an arranged marriage had been spoken of sometime earlier. No one knew this other family except her father, John Catalano.

It was said that the absent suitor was a bit older than Rosina; it was also reported that he would be coming to America with funds to start a business. The Catalano brothers were always in Rosina's presence so there was little opportunity for a boy to ask about this mysterious suitor.

My father told his brother that there were two reasons that he never dared to pinch Rosina: first, she was too special to flirt with, and secondly…he knew he would be in trouble with her brothers. *He only shared this topic with me when I was a grown man and we discussed such amusing things. Apparently he then felt that I would not be judgmental concerning his youthful behavior.*

At one point, Mike asked his brother if he thought their mother knew about their flirtatious pinching. Roy laughed and said that he was sure that she knew because 'she knew everything that went on,' but he assured his brother that she was never going to pose the topic to them because she knew all about the ways of young Italian men.

Michael saw a profound change in his mother after arriving in America and…especially after giving birth to his third sister. He did not believe that the births had anything to do with this change, however. He remembered his mother being a quiet woman of few words when there was just the three of them in Calabria.

Now Elizabeth was outspoken and often dictated issues to her husband in a manner that would have never been thought of. She avoided using this new dominant power on her sons, however. She did not actually dote on them, but she saw to it that they had whatever they needed to appear prominent in the eyes of their peers.

Elizabeth was the one responsible for bartering the music lessons for the boys. And even during her illness, she managed to see that her sons had pressed shirts when they went out and she reminded them to have their hair combed and shoes shined.

I didn't realize, as I was growing up, that those two prerequisites in leaving the house, which was a constant reminder by my father, were an extension of his mother. "Boys," he would say, "Be sure to have your hair combed and shoes shined when you leave the house!" He never actually inspected us before our departure, but would remind us repeatedly so that it was ingrained in our minds to do so.

In his journal, my father admitted that he did make an attempt to reach Rosina through her brothers, but they were not especially interested in conveying his interest. Their family had come from the northern part of Calabria; it was a town near the city of Naples, although still in the Calabrian region. At that time, northerners frowned upon those from the south of Italy. Class differences meant something and the southern Italians were the poorest of the poor and assumed to be less intelligent based on their limited exposure to formal education.

As a young boy, I heard my mother cast up to my father that she was aware that he had a crush on Rosie, but my father would never acknowledge that such a crush had existed. It was not until reading his entry in the journal that I knew that my mother was right. Perhaps my father never wanted his children to know that an earlier interest existed before meeting my mother.

In my father's diary he wrote a short note about Rosina, stating that he was not familiar with the warm rush that he felt in her presence. A few of his other sentences led me to believe that he had not yet responded to the usual feelings that accompany adolescence and the male hormones. But apparently Rosina had brought forth the hidden or latent feelings of manhood in him.

Chapter 13

A Marriage takes place

While my father was getting nowhere with his crush on Rosina Catalano, his brother was moving ahead with intentions of marriage. The year was 1920 and Roy had been dating a girl whose family was well known to Elizabeth. The couple met six months earlier and this time Roy was not going to play and get away. Nervina Rizzo had her eye on Roy for some months earlier but had never been able to find a time or circumstance that brought them together.

The changing conditions of the family and those conditions placing more demands on the brothers' work schedule was not allowing for leisure time. It was a constant cycle of work in the mines, working in the family store and attending to other necessary family chores that eliminated the previous social time in which the brothers had indulged.

During this same time, Nervina had been doing her homework on the comings and goings of the older brother. She was known to like a good time and her personality showed that to be obvious. She was not a shy girl and the brothers were usually attracted to the somewhat shy girls who were really 'closet flirts!' Since there was nothing shy about Nervina, rather than opposites attracting, it was going to be 'two peas of the same pod!'

Elizabeth was well aware of Nervina's interest in her son, but was not concerned because she was friends with the Rizzo family and had gotten to know their daughter. She knew that they kept

Nervina in check. Her parents had not held firm to Old World traditions that made it impossible for girls of Italian families to enjoy a social life before marriage, but it was still important for Italian girls to adhere to social practices that assured that they could be 'marketed' as virgins.

A non-virgin brought too much disgrace to an Italian family, so there was lots of flirting and a lot more pinching, but there was a limit to the Italian behavior. If anything was going to progress beyond the harmless flirting it had to be outside of Italian families; the cost within was too great and…too expensive to consider.

When Roy and Nervina began dating, the mothers were well aware of the relationship; it was not being done in secret. Both families were not of the strict Southern Italian culture that would later confront my father. But they were also preparing the couple to walk down the aisle because at that time there was no such thing as 'casual dating' among Italian families. And so, in the late summer of 1920, Roy and Nervina married with the blessings of both families.

Although the mothers had orchestrated the union, the couple believed that the flirting and attraction had been all of their own doing. Elizabeth knew that her oldest son was marrying into a good family and Nervina's family was pleased to have become a part of the Albano-Alberto family. Nervina's mother was aware that Elizabeth Trippodi had come from a family of musicians… accomplished musicians. And as we shall learn, Dominic's family could claim artistic pride because of the renowned sculptor, Salvatore Albano.

Michael did not stand for his brother because it had been agreed upon that one of Nervina's several brothers were due that honor. Like Rosina Catalano, she was the only daughter among several brothers. In 1921, almost nine months to the day, Nervina gave birth to their first child; it was a boy and he was named

Samuel. I must admit that I was never aware of a different Italian name because we called him Sammy and later: Buddy. But I would guess that his birth name might have had a more Italian 'ring' to it than Samuel…perhaps Salvatore.

Shortly after his marriage to Nervina, (later known to family and friends as Nervie), Roy was determined to find a bride for his brother. After all, the brothers seldom enjoyed the pleasures of life singularly and this was no exception.

Roy repeatedly told his brother how happy he was and that he wanted him to experience this same happiness. "Besides," Roy had poked, "you have to catch up with me in making babies!" My father reminded his brother that he would have to find a wife before he could enter that contest!

During that same year that Roy's first child was born, another event occurred that would close the chapter on the dream that was to end…Michael Corina arrived from Italy and shortly thereafter, the marriage took place between him and Rosina Catalano.

My father was invited to the wedding as an extension of the invitation that Roy and Nervie received and he was welcomed by Rosina, who introduced him to her husband. Michael Corina a/k/a Mike Corina was never known by an Italian version of that name, but had arrived in this country (or perhaps leaving Ellis Island) with the name Michael.

Later, during the celebration and while some families were dancing, Rosina walked up to my father and took him aside. "She spoke very softly to me," he wrote, "and told me that she was aware of my interest in her but she did not respond because she knew that it would not be fair to encourage me when her marriage had been arranged years earlier and she had been corresponding through letters with Michael Corina." I would suggest that that conversation may have put closure to the crush.

During that same intimate conversation, my father adds in his diary that Rosina told him that she considered him a very nice gentleman and that he was going to make a wonderful husband for the right girl. It would have seemed like a 'brush-off' if she had said that in an earlier conversation, but now that this was being told to him at the time of her wedding he accepted it as a sincere compliment. *In years to follow, my parents would become close friends of the Corinas.*

Now Michael was left to navigate the social waters alone; his best friend, his brother, was married and a father of a son. And Rosina, his teenage crush, was married and so it ended a chapter in his life.

Chapter 14
A Chain of Events

Both Michael and Roy continued to work the mines, but now it was primarily my father who tended the family store. His brother had to spend time with his new family, although he did try to show up occasionally to give a hand and to pay attention to their parents. By now, both parents were in need of constant medical attention and there were three sisters to care for. This added responsibility brought about the demands usually known to that of a married man, but without the pleasures of a wife.

I never knew the age of my grandparents, but assuming that Elizabeth was a young bride when she married Rocco Scolari, she would have been in her late thirties when she gave birth to their last daughter. Today, that would not pose a problem with most pregnancies, but apparently her health began deteriorating during her last pregnancy. At that time, late pregnancies were considered to be of a higher risk since less was known about treating complications in those pregnancies.

My father was not aware, at the time, that there were plans at work by Roy in finding him a suitable wife. The brothers had always enjoyed the same social pleasures and now Roy felt that he was enjoying the happiness of marriage which his brother should also experience and enjoy. Much of the discussions were being done very quietly, but there was definitely a movement in the works and the number of individuals involved lent itself to an old fashion tale from a Gothic novel. Since most of the families migrating from Calabria were connected in one way or another, it was no surprise that Nervina's family was distant cousins with the Catalano family and the Catalano family, on the other side, was related to a family near Punxsutawney in the small Italian village of Walston. (The town had become known through families who were working in coal mines nearby and later those immigrants who were lucky enough to find employment in the steel mills of Pittsburgh; those workers who eventually worked in the steel mills would commute on weekends and share sleeping rooms much like the Mexican workers are known to do today).

Nervina was friends with Frank Catalano's wife and Frank mentioned that his distant cousin had a daughter who might now be of marrying age. He told his wife that Roy might want to look into that possibility for his brother Mike.

The several conversations were taking place without my father's knowledge. Roy wanted to ascertain whether this girl was already spoken for and/or if she was of the age of marriage before sharing his findings with my father.

There was no actual age for marriage, but it was assumed that a girl who had reached the stage of womanhood, whether that be fifteen, sixteen or seventeen, would be a candidate for marriage, if…the father consented to releasing his daughter at that given age.

This project brought Frank Catalano and my Uncle Roy closer since they were going to be the chief architects of this plot. Frank wrote a letter to John DeFazio inquiring about his family and asking how the individual children were. Frank's family was related to John's wife, Filomena, but the letter had to be directed to the husband of the family. John DeFazio wrote back indicating the ages of his children and sure enough, his daughter Maria Lucia had reached her sixteenth birthday.

I realize that the chain of relations that was just described might seem to be like an impossible maze of characters, but one must *remember that this was a very accepted manner in which to secure a bride during that time in the Italian culture. And…we must keep in mind that distant cousins were **cousins** and very little distinction was made as to whether that individual was a first, second, or third cousin.*

At this stage of the orchestrated production, Michael was brought in on the plan. Roy told him that he might have found the right girl for his shy brother. He continued by warning my father that there could be no pinching going on with this girl. Michael's face lit up and he assured his brother that he knew better than to conduct himself in that way with a stranger's daughter!

One does not have to grow up in a society in order to inherit the sexual mores of that society or culture. And the brothers had inherited the 'Russian hands and Roman fingers' of their Italian ancestors… although that culture was largely practiced in another continent.

A second letter was sent by Frank Catalano expressing a desire for the Albano/Alberto brothers to pay their respects to his family with a visit. With this letter, there was little doubt in John DeFazio's mind as to what was at work. Now he had to think hard on whether to encourage such a visit. He decided to allow the visit, but was in no way accepting what might come about from that visit. It would just be the first such visit that he had allowed to his home.

Of his five children, John DeFazio's daughter Maria Lucia was his oldest—his first born. She had served as an important aid to his wife, Filomena, who had endured many pregnancies—several of those being failed pregnancies. Nevertheless, he knew the day would come when this visit would be requested by one of the Italian families who had come from the Old Country.

In John's mind, there was never going to be any other visits granted other than by a reputable Italian family—and John did his own bit of research to learn of the Albano family and their origins.

John and Filomena had been married in the small village of Motta Santa Lucia near the city of Catanzaro, the regional capital city of Calabria. John had worked in the Pennsylvania coal mines since their arrival in the New World and was quietly pleased to learn that the brothers who had requested this special visit also worked the mines since the family's arrival from Calabria. He did not intend to make his inquiry known upon their visit, however.

The visit was not quickly agreed upon. There was a lapse of time between the letter requesting that visit and a response. Mike and Roy were both on edge awaiting the reply.

Almost a month later, a letter was sent to Frank explaining that there were many happenings between work in the mines and preparations for the upcoming Christmas holy days that prevented a quicker response.

The reasons given were obviously of little validity since Christmas was still months away. The slow and nonchalant reply suggested that this was not going to be an easy project; they were going up against another Calabrian and he was going to control the movements on that chess board!

My father told me that he was ready to 'throw in the towel' and shop elsewhere. He used that terminology because now, years later, he could look back on the entire transaction with some humor… especially when my mother was nearby hearing the story being related to me. During that same discussion with my father, he explained the importance of only considering a virgin as a bride.

I found it strange that my father had used the word 'shopping' when referring to his search for a wife. *I guess that since today's social media offers so many dating services, one could view that method as 'shopping' also! But of course such methods were not considered at that time.*

He told me that when an Italian man bought a new suit (*of course this was years after poverty had been present in his life*), a man would always shop for the finest silk and wasn't content to accept other fabrics or used merchandise. He said that was the same in seeking a wife, and he went on to assure me that when he met my mother he knew he had been introduced to that finest silk. *He made certain that my mother heard this explanation! He constantly tried to flirt by flattering her.*

The meeting finally took place in late October and the brothers were nervous! Elizabeth couldn't understand why they should be so anxious. She told her sons that it should be the girl who was anxious when she was being visited by such a handsome and talented boy as her son. *You should know that Italian men are always referred to as boys by their parents, but men by their wives*!

Chapter 15
The Audition

Elizabeth reluctantly helped her sons prepare for the visit, which of course all parties realized was 'the audition.' She was not reluctant to help because she wanted to deny her sons, but she could not see the necessity of her sons going through this ordeal. Dominic reminded her that this was only in keeping with the Italian tradition of protecting the daughter's integrity and… perhaps more importantly maintaining the respect and honor of the family name.

Dominic reminded her that she had forgotten the traditions of the 'Old World' and perhaps was becoming Americanized too quickly. She did not appreciate his comment, but remained unresponsive. Since her boys were intent on achieving success, she was determined to see to it that there would be no disappointment. It was obvious from her demeanor, however, that she resented any girl putting her son through this anxiety.

Yes, Elizabeth was aware that it was a tradition that many 'Old World' countries followed—especially the countries bordering the Mediterranean. But when it came to her sons, she wanted to forget tradition and get on with her son establishing his role as a husband.

There was no audition for Roy; they had made their own way together to reach the conclusion of marriage. And now her youngest son, Michael, was having to go through this terrible process. That resentment remained with Elizabeth into the marriage.

The Other Marconi

Dominic suggested that the boys bring John DeFazio a pouch of tobacco and Elizabeth reluctantly suggested that perhaps some flowers would be appropriate for his wife.

I'm not sure how Dominic gained knowledge that John DeFazio smoked a pipe, but I suppose that he had made his own inquiries through Frank Catalano. So there was some tobacco from the store placed in a small pouch. And of course the boys were reminded more than a few times to have their hair combed and their shoes polished when they arrived. They were advised to check them before their arrival in the event that some last-minute attention was necessary (a spare large miner's hankie was tucked inside of Roy's front pocket for such a necessity).

Transportation for this important journey was arranged through Nervie's uncle and so when the day arrived, the uncle and the boys were off for Walston, a three and half hour road trip (during that time). The boys' suits were pressed and creased military style.

Both Mike and Roy were meticulously shaven, but with some care to show that both men were capable of facial hair growth; this was an important issue so as not to appear in any way less than fully matured. Facial hair, even then, was a sign of masculinity and maturity and so a proper trimming…but not total removal was suggested! Nothing was left to chance, but little did they know that nothing was going to satisfy John DeFazio on this initial visit.

The men were unaware that rather than an audition, this was going to be a stern interview or…perhaps more closely related to an Inquisition!

Roy knew that his brother was going to be nervous about the meeting and so he suggested that he do most of the talking and that my father should speak only when DeFazio was addressing him directly.

John DeFazio did not disappoint the brothers. He was only slightly cordial to the men and showed a minimum of Italian courtesy and hospitality. This was evident by the well planned reception which consisted of coffee and freshly baked sweet bread… but nothing more! There was none of John's homemade wine or fruit or meats or cheeses or any of the fare that is commonly shown when an Italian family is receiving another of theirs for a formal visit. It was the very least of treats that is offered a *stranieri italiano*!

Upon offering the gifts that were so carefully planned: the flowers and the pipe tobacco, Filomena was summoned from her kitchen to accept the flowers and then disappeared back into her place…the kitchen. There was no evidence of their daughter, Maria Lucia. However, she was also in the kitchen waiting to learn if her father was going to summon her for some reason…any reason. But that never happened.

The meeting went well with Michael answering the few questions that were directed to him. There was a slight 'breaking of the ice' when the conversation moved to mining. Of course John DeFazio knew that these boys were also miners, but he never admitted to being aware of that fact. Actually, his manner of entering that subject did serve to open a more comfortable dialogue between the men.

When the visit ended, Roy took the initiative to ask if it were possible to return at some later time. He told John that they would be very pleased if they could meet his daughter Maria Lucia. John almost bolted with Roy's boldness, but then realized that this was the reason for the visit in the first place, and of course he was going to have to give an answer…but that answer could have been negative or affirmative.

Michael's face gleamed with delight when Lucia's father indicated that a second visit was possible, but that it could not be set at this particular time.

I found an entry in my father's black book that referred to that initial meeting with my mother's father. It was located about midway into the diary. It was almost a confession as much as an admittance. And it wasn't written as though it was meant to be read by me or… perhaps anyone!

"I'll never forget my first meeting with Lucy's father," he wrote. "I never thought I could fear anything more than I did my first time in the mines, but I found that first visit with my father-in-law to surpass that fear. I've never admitted to that fear of going down into the 'black hole,' because I knew that I couldn't. My brother Roy had already been down there many times and I knew that I could not disappoint my father; he had been down that hole hundreds of times."

My father never spoke of a fear of the mineshaft, but only his contempt for it because of near tragedy that occurred subsequent to this period of time. That near tragedy will soon be revealed.

I found that the entries were not always in chronological order, but I learned to put the pieces to the puzzle where they belonged. He wrote a bit more about that first meeting with John DeFazio. "I wasn't sure that I would ever be grateful for those days in the mines, but it definitely played a part in gaining acceptance from Lucy's father. Perhaps that first meeting even prepared me for job interviews because nothing was as rigid and filled with anxiety as that meeting; and I shall always be indebted to my brother Roy for being there for me."

It was just another of many reasons that my father felt so close to his brother and remained so for their entire lives.

The Dream

My father never shared his dreams with me, but apparently he did share some of them with his brother—and why not? The brothers were practically 'joined at the hip' in their closeness to each other during their youth and even into their young adult lives. One significant dream that he shared with Roy showed up in that black book—that same book that served as his diary. The dream occurred shortly after the initial visit to the home of John DeFazio.

You may recall the incident that had occurred some years earlier in their village of Oppido Mamertina: Guido Costello's theft of Mrs. Fortino's chicken. Well, my father had a frightening dream that while John DeFazio stepped out of the living room and into the kitchen to speak to his wife (which never happened), Lucia appeared for a short time in his presence and he could not resist the desire to pinch her buttocks. Suddenly, John DeFazio appeared in front of him with sharp piercing eyes and a sharp blade to match his eyes. He spared no time in chopping off the fingers that had pinched his daughter. Michael told his brother that immediately after his fingers were cut at the knuckles, he awoke in a cold sweat.

His brother Roy laughed and assured him that he still had all of his fingers and that he had read too much into the performance that Lucia's father had given. Michael recalls his brother suggesting what a match it would make to put their mother into a room with John DeFazio; he likened it to orchestrating a rooster fight. The idea of such a match brought a laugh from my father and he forgot the dream shortly thereafter.

The brothers weren't aware that once they left the DeFazio residence, John admitted to himself and…only to himself…that he was quite pleased with the young man who had come to apply for the role of his son-in-law.

He later made it known in a very quiet and subtle way that he was pleased with the respect that was shown him by the young man. He also realized the role that the older brother played; it reminded him of the way things were in their homeland of Italia… and especially within that region known as Calabria.

Unfortunately, Filomena was never privy to these thoughts. In many Italian homes, it was not information that the wife was entitled to learn from her husband. And while Filomena knew that her daughter had feelings for another within their small village, she never knew if those feelings had been expressed or acknowledged by the young man since daughters and sons had little or no say in these matters of the heart.

My father told me that his mother was not so pleased with the obvious grilling that her sons had endured. She knew that custom was being followed but she, nevertheless, resented the fact that her son had to be the victim of that custom.

He recalled Elizabeth mumbling something in a dialect, one of which he was unfamiliar. But he knew that whatever she said, was not flattering concerning John DeFazio! Elizabeth's contempt for John DeFazio continued to grow and…grow into her son's eventual marriage.

My father was concerned that this contempt could create future problems if, in fact, Lucia became his bride. (*This might be the appropriate time to explain that most daughters born to Italian-Catholic families carried the first name of Mary, the Blessed Mother, and then were given a second name that would eventually become the name by which they were known. Thus, Maria Lucia would be called Lucia and later adopted the Anglicized name of Lucy*).

Michael overheard his parents talking in the kitchen one day and heard his father remind his mother that their son must be patient and look forward to the second visit. He told me that he remembered hearing his father say that 'he was confident that I was in good hands with my brother Roy.'

Photo of John DeFazio and his young family
Lucia, as a child, shown wearing her baptismal dress

Chapter 16

The Waiting Game

Roy warned his brother that they must wait before requesting the second visit. Although they had let the door open for John DeFazio to extend that second visit to them, he was quite sure that it would never come unless they took the initiative. But that initiative must not be too soon or it might appear to show signs of anxiety. They did not want to give John DeFazio reason to believe that my father was desperate to find a bride.

It was really a 'cat and mouse' game of almost asking, "Who blinks first?" Of course Roy knew that he had to do the 'blinking,' and this time the letter would come directly from him, rather than from Frank Catalano.

After a first request was denied due to holidays and such, a second letter requesting the visit was acknowledged and a date was set just prior to the Easter holiday. It was now early spring of 1922 and there would be no mistaking the purpose for the visit and the subsequent results that were expected.

Dominic played a hand in preparing his sons for this all-important visit. Elizabeth had decided that she wanted no part of this plan; she thought that her husband was going overboard, and she was going to leave the preparations in his hands. He had ordered a fine piece of silk from his store supplier that would make a beautiful shawl for Lucia's mother. Dominic also ordered a special blend of pipe tobacco which should certainly gain favor with the father (the tobacco was placed in an attractive leather pouch)—all of this preparation for seeking a bride who had not yet been seen!

It should be noted that since the initial visit, John DeFazio's daughter had celebrated her seventeenth birthday on December fifth of the previous year.

My father knew that progress was being made because he told me that this meeting went exceptionally well. How could he tell, he asked rhetorically...? Shortly after their arrival, John DeFazio called his wife from the kitchen and asked her why she had not finished setting the table with meats and cheeses and some of his special wine?

Poor Filomena was left in the dark by this sudden summons! There had been no discussion of meats and cheeses and her husband's homemade wine. But she knew where to gain access to these luxury items; it was in their cold cellar below the house. She scurried back into the kitchen instructing Lucia to go to the cold cellar and bring back these precious holiday items.

I'm told that my mother made a bold move. She decided that it was time that she saw this mysterious suitor, so she quickly glanced around the corner of the kitchen doorway. She was unaware of the plot that her mother would initiate for her. Once the goods were brought up from the cellar, her mother instructed her to set the table with the necessary dishes and utensils for serving.

John was taken aback when his daughter appeared in the living room rather than his wife; there had been no permission given by him for this entrance! He would have been furious except that he realized that at some time during this visit he was going to have to bring his daughter out of hiding. It just wasn't supposed to happen like this! So he took the opportunity to say, "Ah, Michele, this is my daughter, Maria Lucia."

My father said he still recalls the red cheeks that were the product of shyness and embarrassment. It was from this initial

The Other Marconi

introduction to my mother that my father gave her the title, "Bashful Lucy." It was at that moment that my father felt a sudden rush…similar to that which he had experienced in the presence of Rosina Catalano.

Once Lucia placed the items on the table she scurried back into the kitchen and whispered to her mother, "He is a nice looking and pleasant man, mama." Filomena was happy to hear some encouragement from her daughter because she knew her heart had been broken by the reality that she could never have her first love, John Farbo. *It was much later into the marriage that both partners learned that the other had experienced 'a crush that was not meant to be.'*

In a sense, this meeting sealed the deal! At the end of this visit, John DeFazio informed the brothers that a future meeting could take place at which time his wife would set up a visit of Michele with his daughter. I'm not sure what the Italian definition for this visit was, but in essence it was a short walk or stroll through the village which would be accompanied by Lucia's godmother, a neighbor woman and Christina Farbo, the wife of the distant cousin of John Farbo (who was the cousin of Frank Catalano's wife and…coincidentally, the mother of John Farbo, Jr., Lucia's secret crush).

The entourage of women was to walk behind the couple to ensure that there was no contact and limited conversation of the purest kind—in other words, no flirtatious comments or anything that could be considered disrespectful to the girl.

"John DeFazio had engaged in previous conversation with my brother," my father wrote, "making sure that he knew the rules that accompanied this **walk**." He wanted assurance from Roy that there would be no disrespect shown by touching or words that suggested familiarity.

It should be noted here that all of the conversation was, of course, in Italian. Although John DeFazio insisted that his children speak

English outside of the home, he himself never learned any English and spoke only his native tongue until the day he died.

Author's note

I was first told about 'the walk' as a teenager. It was years later that "The Godfather" motion picture was introduced to cinemas throughout our country. I was surprised to see a similar *walk* being shown as part of the protocol prior to the Sicilian wedding. I realized that much research had been done in preparation for that movie.

The ceremonial "walk" took place about a month after the second meeting and my parents were married on August 14, 1922.

Michael learned quickly about the games that parents often play and the sometimes unreasonable customs that were the norm in an Italian society. He began to also make comparisons between his mother and his new father-in-law. He was also able to compare the compassionate side of his father with that of poor Filomena, whose eyes were full of both love and sadness.

It was revealed in later tales of the hard life Filomena had endured as John DeFazio's wife. If there had been any trace of romanticism in that marriage, it was abandoned in Catanzaro and died before the couple ever reached America.

Before we go forward, however, it should be noted that a secret that was kept hidden for years was revealed in my father's journal: secret letters that passed between my father and mother following the second meeting and prior to "the walk." Lucy had managed to place a note somewhere within the table setting of my father's service ware or plate.

If that secret had been revealed to her father it is not certain who would have suffered a greater punishment: Lucia or her mother! Filomena had been the victim of many acts of spousal abuse during their marriage, and the lack of discipline from a daughter would have been blamed on the mother.

I am personally aware of a situation many years later, and as a teenager, within another Italian family when the youngest of the daughters became pregnant before her wedding day. The father refused to speak to his wife for nearly a year in order to punish her for failing to instill better moral standards in their daughter. This cruel and unjust punishment had been exacted towards the innocent wife in the early 1950's…and not in the early days of that century. Some *Old World* customs were not easily abandoned.

Perhaps John DeFazio would have not punished his wife for a year, but the back of his hand might have easily found way to his wife's frail cheek. However, the letters did remain a secret and I was privy to only one that had been carefully preserved in the dresser drawer of my mother. It was in Italian and so I will offer it first as it was written and then I shall translate it for my readers:

> *Cara Lucia,*
>   *mia timida Lucia, ho aspettato tanto tempo per trovarvi. Grazie per avermi dato il piacere e l'onore di ricevere il Vostro indirizzo che mi permette di scrivere questa lettera.*
>   *Seguo le Vostre istruzioni e spedisco questa ed altre lettere alla Vostra amica e confidente Tessa Fabro. Non vedo l'ora della prossima passeggiata, Vi penso sempre e di continuo; anche se non cercherò di prendere la Vostra mano, sappiate che il mio cuore la sta tenendo stretta in ogni passo.*
>   *Lucia, spero con tutto il cuore che Voi accettate di essere mia moglie.*
> *A presto,*
> *Michele*

And below is the nearest translation that I can offer to my readers:

Dear Lucia,

My shy Lucia, I waited so long to find you. Thank you for giving me the pleasure and the honor to receive your address which allows me to write this letter.

I follow your instructions and send this and other letters to your friend and confidant Tessa Farbo.

I will think of you every day and every hour until our Walk. And since I will not try to take your hand, please know that my heart is touching your hand with every step of our walk.

Lucia, I hope with all my heart that you will agree to be my wife.

See you soon,
Michele

I have learned from my father's journal that there were other letters before their marriage, but I do not have access to them and am not sure if they were saved.

Later in my story, I will share a part of that journal with my readers, although the journal sometimes contradicts stories that were told to me by my father. I can only guess that since the journal was written near the end of my father's life, during a time when he was struggling with the dreaded disease of Parkinson's, there may have been some areas of his early life that were now distorted or partially forgotten. The small black book that I've considered his diary, however, seems to be very much in line with many of the earlier stories he chose to share with me.

PHOTO OF WEDDING PICTURE

Chapter 17
Elizabeth's Revenge

The following story was told to me by my mother and later, shamefully confirmed by my father. It was an event that almost cost Michael his marriage and occurred on their *honeymoon*: it was the day following their vows, although in the real sense of the word…there was no honeymoon!

The wedding had taken place in Walston and the wedding mass had been celebrated at the small church at the bottom of the hill known as St. Anthony's. It had been a lovely ceremony and Roy stood for his brother, while one of the women from the small village of Walston stood for Lucia. All of the women who had participated in the 'walk' were also present at the church.

But after the ceremony, it was only family members who returned to the bride's home. It was later learned that those same women from the *walk* had helped Filomena prepare the wedding dinner, while John DeFazio proudly presented his homemade wine.

It was understood that the couple would live with my father's parents for a period of time. That period had not been defined, but shortly thereafter it was defined by my mother—in part due to the 'morning after' event.

Elizabeth only waited until she heard sounds from her son's matrimonial bedroom. Perhaps she counted the minutes before she would make her entrance; she had to be sure that she had allowed sufficient time to be fair in her investigation. So it may have been within half an hour of hearing some sounds through the paper-thin walls that separated the kitchen from that matrimonial chamber.

Suddenly, without any warning…not a knock on the door or a sound of warning, she opened the door and told the couple to "get out," to immediately leave the room! Both Michael and his bride were in shock. They grabbed a few pieces of clothing and were into the kitchen in a matter of minutes. What was the purpose of this terrible intrusion, they wondered?

Lucia had not been prepared for this outburst, or had she? It was minutes later that she remembered the warning that her mother had given her. Elizabeth and her eldest daughter, Mary, entered the bedroom and slammed the door shut behind them.

When Elizabeth returned from the bridal chamber with a sheet in her hands and a smile on her face the couple stood with shock and embarrassment. Michael's mother said that everything was okay, they could begin their breakfast now. The bedsheet contained blood spots from the marital act of sexual intercourse. She had confirmed that her daughter-in-law was a virgin!

Later that morning, my father heard his parents having words over the bedroom inspection. His compassionate father had scolded his wife saying that she had ruined their son's first day of marriage. Elizabeth was heard saying, "I don't care. I am not going to have a *putann* marrying my son. He had to go through hell to get her and I wanted to make sure that it was worth all of the effort that he and his brother put into it."

My father had avoided going to his mother about this embarrassment to him and his wife. But in his diary he wrote that he had consulted his father asking why she would do this to them when that same standard had not been demanded of his brother's wife.

When his mother learned of this conversation, she assured her son that she would have conducted the same inspection of Nervina if they had spent their wedding night in their home. She also assured my father that she had known the Rizzo family and was confident that they had monitored their daughter's behavior to meet the Italian standards. She continued to say that she didn't know the DeFazios. "Besides," she told him, "Nervina's parents didn't put your brother through hell; he didn't have to walk on hot coals to get her!"

That episode was the very rocky beginning for my parents. My mother wanted to return to her family. She told my father that she was not going to stay in a house with such mistrust. Michael apologized for his mother and assured his new bride that he would never allow his mother to insult her again. (He made that promise, however, knowing that he could never keep it because he knew that he didn't have the power nor the will to control his mother's behavior…especially on such matters).

Years later, this 'morning after' story was repeated to my wife shortly after our marriage. I recall my father being somewhat embarrassed to have it repeated. But then, he took me aside as a newly married man and explained what a terrible situation he had found himself in at the time. How could he show anger towards his mother? And, at the same time, he told me that he was genuinely worried that his new bride would not agree to remain with his parents for even a second night. He had to walk a tight rope in appeasing both women. He had never shown disrespect towards his mother; he never recalled raising his voice to her. It just wasn't done!

PHOTO OF ELIZABETH

Chapter 18

A Marriage in Progress

Michael did not have the luxury of remaining with his parents as long as was originally planned after that bedroom intrusion. Lucia had threatened to make good on her plan to return home to her parents if she had to endure intrusions into their privacy and being subjected to hostility by his mother. Of course she may have not realized that her father would have never allowed it. She now belonged to Michael just as Filomena 'belonged' to him!

My father discovered quite soon after his marriage to my mother that the shy, bashful girl that he had first witnessed during the visits to the DeFazio residence had inherited the tenacity of her father, rather than the fragile demeanor of her mother. He did not admit to her, however, the added attractiveness that he found in this assertiveness.

Perhaps he had inherited from his father the appeal that an assertive woman could bring to a marriage, although he had never discussed those Freudian attractions with his father; such conversations were verboten!

My father and his brother continued working in the coal mines after they were married, but both brothers were seeking other employment so that they could begin a future for their new families. And Roy's wife was expecting their second child. Thereafter, it seemed that there was never a year that she was not pregnant, but there was a miscarriage that occurred somewhere

The Other Marconi

during the first five years of their marriage. It didn't seem to stop the cycle of childbirths by her, however.

Within four months of their marriage, my parents moved to their own small living quarters. My father had managed to put enough funds together to rent a small house not far from his parents, but out of sight and sound from his watchful mother. And on August 2nd of the following year, Lucia gave birth to their first child, a daughter, who they named Elizabeth.

As tradition dictated, it was agreed upon that the first daughter would honor the name of his mother. A second daughter would be named Filomena, but if it were a boy my mother insisted that the child bear the name of my father. Now the race began!

Chapter 19
A Time for Celebration

There is little that has been said about the private music lessons that were arranged by Elizabeth for her sons, but there is reason to say more. The brothers took their lessons quite seriously and became good at their instruments: Roy at the horn and my father at the slide trombone.

The brothers had joined a local band; and it should be noted that the affiliation with the band came before either of the brothers had married. But Roy's wife wasn't too keen on the band membership; she was fiercely jealous of Roy and his popularity as a single man had warranted her concern.

Michael did not mention his musical talent during 'the interview' with John DeFazio; he wasn't sure if that would be a plus or minus during that *inquisition* so the brothers had agreed to leave that out of the *resumé*. It was probably a good idea since his future father-in-law had vetted him like someone applying for mine supervisor! Michael was pleased to learn that, at least initially, his bride was proud that her handsome husband was musically talented. Later, that pride would become lost in a mutual concern with her sister-in-law over the exposure that these young Italian men had with the female audience that so much adored the musical duo.

In 1923 Calvin Coolidge became president of the United States upon the sudden death of President Warren Harding, and the band in which the brothers played had been invited to play for

The Other Marconi

the inauguration. It was an honor that my father never forgot. I'm told that if you wanted to see two grown men behave like children who had just received everything they ever wanted for Christmas, well…that was the reaction of Elizabeth's sons when they were made aware of the band's invitation.

Of course both Dominic and Elizabeth were popping with pride and why not? Here was a family that came from poor beginnings, from the lowest financial rung of Italian society and now their sons would play in the band that was honoring the President of The United States.

One had to be of Italian heritage to realize what music meant to their culture. And now…to be honored with this distinction was going to feed the *Italian Boys'* ego beyond one could imagine. "Now what will John DeFazio have to say about his famous son-in-law?" was words echoed by Elizabeth on more than one occasion.

The inauguration was taking place the day following the birth of my sister Elizabeth and that created some concern…the fact that my father would not be by my mother's side during the first days of her birth created anxiety and disappointment. But Lucy knew how much this meant to the brothers and decided that she had to overlook the conflict of events. I'm told that the conversation went something like this: "But Lu, how could anyone have known that Harding was going to die and interfere with our daughter's birth?"

From time to time my mother would hear this same sort of defense when Michael was scheduled to play with the band during future conflicts of events. Of course it wasn't about a president's death in the subsequent situations.

After a few lines of defense, it became obvious to both brothers that they were going to have to give up the band! Their wives had banned together to read them the 'riot act' and it was usually concerning where the men were going to spend their night sleeping. For two young women who had grown up knowing the

Old Italian ways, they quickly learned as savvy wives what worked in controlling their men!

I asked my father why more had not been told to me and my siblings about his days in the band and how he found time to learn to play his instrument. I knew that he was pleased by my inquiry because he gave me some detailed background on the topic of the music lessons.

His mother, Elizabeth Trippodi, was of a family originally from Puglia and several of her cousins were accomplished musicians. I believe that one of her cousins was Concert Master of a well-respected orchestra at the time.

There was additional artistic reason for this family to be proud of their heritage and their ancestry on my father's side; and it was revealed in my father's journal. He wrote that his grandfather, Michele Albano, was cousins with a young man whose name was Salvatore Albano, born in Oppido Mamertina in 1841. He began in Calabria as a sculptor of wooden Presepi or Nativity scenes. Because of his talent, his townspeople gave him a stipend to study in Naples.

My father recounted the story in his journal in a slightly different way:

"My grandfather's trade was making chairs and barrels. He and his brother both went to the woods to get lumber. Well my grandfather and his cousin, Salvatore Albano, use to take a bunch to their father. On the way to the woods Salvatore used to stop at a place where there was clay and he made statues of kings, saints and so on. A priest took interest on what Salvatore was doing and he ask the parents if he could send Salvatore to Napoli or Roma to a school of arts. Oh, yes, Salvatore went and became artist and made a Madonna and got the 1st prize. Later King Victor Emanuel of Italy appointed him as Senator of Florence, Italy. When visiting his hometown my grandfather Michael used to take little Dominic with him to see his cousin Salvatore. Salvatore took little boy by the hand and said to my grandfather, don't worry I have Dominic follow my footsteps. But Salvatore only lived a few years and died as a bachelor."

In honoring my father's memory, I have copied this particular entry verbatim, only inserting a few commas and even allowing the spelling to remain as it was in the original journal. Although my father's recollection of the story is slightly different than that shown in the records, it may still represent the true story of my great-grandfather's association with the renowned cousin, Salvatore Albano.

Even the public records show two different birth years for my distant cousin; one shows his birth as being 1839, while in the same page of information another birth date is given as 1841. Of course if Salvatore Albano was born in 1839, it would have been exactly a century before my own birth.

But in answer to my question regarding the fact that not much had ever been said about his days of playing in the band, I'm not sure I ever did get a definitive answer. I believe he did indicate that it was a long time ago and after enjoying the births of his children and realizing the responsibility of supporting a family his interest in recalling his band days was minimalized.

Nevertheless, as I have mentioned in another chapter, my father's interest in opera only grew through the years rather than subsiding like his own musical endeavors. I cannot help but to think that his interest in opera grew because he knew that he had a son with whom to share that love of music. More will be told about that common interest at a later time.

Eugenio Michael Albano

About The Music Lessons

Shortly after moving to Morrisdale and locating a sizeable rental property, Elizabeth and Dominic decided to take in boarders to help pay for the house expenses.

Elizabeth learned of a man whose story was known by others in the community; his name was professor Amato. It was not known if he held the credentials for that title, but he was taking on a new position at the school to teach mathematics and music. *At that time in our history, any well-educated person who taught music was distinguished with the title professore or the female version of that title which would be professora.*

Professor Amato and his wife had come to America several years earlier to start a new life for themselves and for their first child who was not yet born. Sadly, his wife and the child died during childbirth.

Amato went back to Italy for a while, but then decided to return to the states to resume his career in teaching. He became a renter of my father's parents and paid a small sum for his room. But in exchange for music lessons, Elizabeth gave him his meals. The other single men, who were miners, did not receive meals with their shared room, but Amato was given 'room and board.'

The bartering system proved to be very advantageous to the brothers who apparently had some natural music talent in their genes. I have arrived at that conclusion because of statements made to me by my father. He told me that both he and his brother found learning to play the instruments effortless. He said that learning to read music was simply like learning a third language, but the language of music was so much more enjoyable.

I asked my father how he found time for music lessons with all the responsibilities he had as a teenager: working the mines, helping his parents at home and learning to read and write good

English. He explained that music was never something that you had to make time for. "It was like having your next meal," he told me. "You knew that it was a part of your daily routine," he said, "and you just figured time for it!"

The brothers really looked forward to the lessons and looked forward to the practice because although they were often practicing separate assignments, it still gave them another common interest and quality time together.

Because of knowing of their constant desire to do things together, I could understand how this project would be a welcomed task, rather than a required one.

Chapter 20

The Families Grow But Not Before Tragedy Strikes

In the early part of 1924, before more joy could be found in the new births of both families, tragedy struck that changed both my father's and my uncle's lives in a bizarre way. One brother's tragedy may have led to the other's good fortune. (That good fortune will occur in a subsequent chapter…good fortune that will lead to my father's career in sales). While the brothers were working the mines together and were in Mine Shaft #9, an explosion occurred that took Roy's left leg. It was unusual that both brothers were not in that same shaft at the time. But Roy had sent my father to go for additional explosives that were in another part of the mine.

When the blast occurred, my father feared that his brother had been taken from him. It was a very traumatic event in their lives. It was obvious from my father's reaction of the accident that these brothers would have given their own lives to save the other. My father never went into detail as to the emotion that he felt, but he did tell me that it was one of the worst days of his life… at least until he found that his brother's life was not taken from him. The explosion completely destroyed most of Roy's left leg, but a successful amputation allowed him to regain his health and be fitted with a prosthesis.

Roy was released from the mines with a small disability pension and my father swore that he would never enter the mines again. However, due to a combination of needing employment and seeking revenge for his brother, my father did re-enter the mines for a period of time shortly thereafter. He was determined that he was going to win out over the evil that had been responsible for the loss of his brother's leg.

Perhaps my father carried with him a sense of vendetta from the Calabrian society because I recall him expressing a type of revenge many times when I was a child. If I stumbled and fell over a loose brick or other protruding object, my father would strike the object with a hammer or remove it from sight and explain that he had punished the object for harming me. Or, if any of us bumped our head on an open cupboard door, he would smack the door as though that was going to lessen the pain we felt from the injury. The protruding object was personified and revenge was exacted!

And so Michael sought revenge by re-entering the mines to prove that he could leave there without the mine shafts taking him. Nevertheless, both wives were relieved that their husbands had left the mines alive, but it was a terrible hardship, both emotionally and financially on the Alberto family.

Later in that same year, a second daughter was born to my parents and a third child was born to Roy and Nervie. Now the Alberto family had a son and two daughters and Roy jokingly reminded his brother, in private, that he would have to work harder to catch up.

When my uncle relayed some of these conversations to me, he told me that my father replied by saying, "Don't let my wife hear you say that or for sure there will be no possibility of a race! She knows I want a boy, so we will keep trying." It was in much later years when we were young adults that we heard some of the shenanigans that went on between the brothers.

During that same period of time, Elizabeth's health was failing and the doctors were not able to give Dominic any encouragement as to a cure. The blood disease that had caused her to almost miscarry her third daughter, Nancy, had re-appeared but with no solution for the illness. I can only assume that she may have suffered from either an advanced anemia or perhaps even leukemia because it was known to be a blood disease.

During those challenging days every member of the family was trying to do his part to support the needs of the family—both financially and emotionally. My father was assuming more responsibility in the day-to-day operation of the grocery store, but with little pay to show for it. Most of the small profits were going for the care of his parents. Dominic was trying to help out in the care of Roy's children while Nervie went back and forth to the hospital also looking after her youngest child.

My parents were trying to figure out what employment my father might be suited for with very little formal education. All of their friends encouraged my father to go into selling because he possessed such an outgoing personality and a sincere interest in others—especially those families who were struggling to assimilate by learning the new English language. And Mike took pride in learning bits and pieces of many languages.

When Roy heard these compliments about his brother while recuperating from the amputation of the battered half of his leg, he showed his brother that he still kept his humor. He took my father aside in his hospital room one day and said, "Yeah Mike, but if those people who know you as a gentlemen knew how much you liked pinching the girls they might not let you talk sweet to the wives when you start selling products.

My uncle always had a good sense of humor and often came up with clever one-liners! He later told me that my father showed some embarrassment and hushed his brother from speaking such things aloud. He was easily embarrassed by his antics of the past.

The Other Marconi

There were several odd jobs that my father took while he tried to find another way to support the family. One of those jobs was making and selling picture frames.

My mother's uncle who lived in Geneva, New York, invited my parents to go to Geneva to see if my father could make a go of selling picture frames there. Geneva was a larger community that had attracted families who could better afford luxuries such as frames for their family photos. There wasn't much of a market for the picture frames among the poor families of coal miners who barely earned enough to feed their families.

My father's notes indicate that he did take a job with a lens company while in Geneva and was paid thirty-five cents an hour. He was also introduced to a gentleman who had some affiliation with the Geneva City Band and played slide trombone with that band for a short period of time.

While my parents were in Geneva, my mother gave birth to their second child, a daughter who was named Filomena, thereby honoring her own dear mother. Shortly thereafter, my parents decided to return to Morrisdale where they would be close to my father's family.

Although Michael was employed in making picture frames and subsequently worked in a lens factory, he had not yet become creative in a way that would later earn him his pseudo name associated with that of the famous Italian inventor. That would come later after more of the family had arrived via the stork! Yes, the baby race between the brothers did continue. And there were several changes that occurred before the family settled into a permanent residence.

Chapter 21

Tragedy Comes in Threes

The families celebrated the return of Mike and Lucy from Geneva. And the small rented house that they had left behind was still vacant and so they moved back into familiar surroundings. But they knew that once a third child entered the family larger quarters were going to be needed. Now my father was holding down two jobs to prepare for the larger family.

It was another August birthday and Mike had his son. And as they planned, the boy was named Michael. There was hardly time for celebration, however, when the dark shadow of tragedy struck. Although the newborn appeared to be a healthy baby, just a week after his birth while the mid-wife was washing the infant, the umbilical cord either ruptured or opened due to faulty attendance at birth.

As the story was told by both of my parents, my mother heard the screams from the mid-wife and rushed in to see her infant son drowning in his blood. All efforts were made to save the child but there was no way of quickly summoning a doctor—most households did not have telephones yet.

By the time a doctor arrived, the child was pronounced dead. *In those days it was common practice for some mid-wives to remain with the new mother to care for the infant for several days or even a week while the mother regained her strength from delivering by natural birth.*

My father told me that it was the worse time in their lives and in their otherwise happy marriage. For months, he said that my mother was awakened by the same dream and screaming, 'please, please save my baby!' My father did his best to comfort her but the loss had emotionally weighed heavily on both of them.

One evening my mother found my father crying in their bedroom…he was crying with such emotion that she feared for his well-being. She heard him saying, "My son…my son is gone." "Why God, would you do this to me? You know how I have waited for a son!"

My father never spoke of that incident, but I am guessing that the concern that my mother had for him helped her to forget some of her own heartbreak. They were both faced with the need to comfort each other. I should note, at this time…that it was only upon reading from my father's diary that I learned just how devastated he had been over the loss of his first son. There are only two instances in my father's life that I had witnessed him crying. It was part of the Old World machismo that didn't allow a man to show his emotions because it was considered a sign of weakness.

In his diary he wrote about the private outbursts of crying that he experienced after the loss of the baby boy. He wrote that he could not afford to let my mother see these outbursts and that because he had to conceal his deep sadness it was all the more painful. He wrote, "…but I had to be strong for dear Lucy…I just had to be!" And so the couple who were married without an opportunity to have romance now found themselves needing each other and sharing the loss of a loved one in a way that brought new meaning into their marriage.

Author's note

In my father's journal he wrote, *"At the time of our baby's death, we were so poor that we didn't have the money to pay for his funeral. My father gave us the money to have that burial."*

I had no idea that my parents struggled financially to that degree during that time in their marriage. The entry also tells me just how much love was expressed from a father who had poor health and was unemployed: my grandfather, Dominic.

A further loss in the family only a few months after the death of baby Michael occurred and perhaps that loss replaced the sadness that they had felt for the loss of their infant son. Elizabeth died just five months after the baby's death, which followed a long illness that began after the birth of her third daughter. Her death was attributed to the rare blood disease (perhaps the blood disease now associated with either advanced anemia or leukemia).

Roy was recuperating and learning to use his new prosthesis. It was made of wood and difficult to manage at the beginning, but he was determined that he would learn to walk with it, and he did. Eventually, he found employment as a clerk in the nearby post office and his wife began to take in washes in order to add to their income. But the 'baby machine' kept going and in 1926 a fourth child was born to Roy and Nervie. But there were no new births for Mike and Lucy that year and there were no more discussions about a baby race between the brothers.

Now there was concern for Dominic since his health was declining and his increased weight since leaving the mines was contributing to his inability to deal with an apparent heart disorder.

Meanwhile, my father's oldest sister, Mary, had married in 1925 at the age of sixteen. She had been writing to a man in Italy who had been introduced to her by a friend (only through letters). The man was just a few years older than Mary and was coming to America to continue his profession as a shoemaker. When he arrived in New Jersey, he sent for her and they were married a few months after she arrived. During those several months she lived with friends of friends of the new husband.

Shortly after Elizabeth's death, Mary and her new husband offered to take in her father to live with them in Jersey. Her husband Joe was doing well with his business. He had come from Italy with the necessary funds to open his own shop, so there was very little, if any, financial struggling that they encountered. Joe was not only a hard worker, but a good manager of his earnings.

The relocation of Dominic was a relief to the families of Mike and Roy as it pertained to their financial responsibility, but he was missed by both sons. At approximately the same time, the two younger sisters decided to move to New Jersey to find employment. And once Rose, my father's second sister married, she and her husband took sister Nancy in to live with them.

In my father's journal I was privy to some personal information that had never before been divulged. Although my grandfather struggled financially after his injuries from the mine that disqualified him from further employment there, as previously noted, it was he who came forth with the funds to pay for the infant son's burial. The entry discloses my father's amazement as to how his father could have saved enough to be so generous.

Chapter 22

Good News Follows and New Additions

1926 was a turning point in my father's life. He had returned to the mines for a short time while he was also selling various items… often door-to-door. But it was in 1926 that he met a banker who took a liking to him. The banker, Mr. Fulton, took notice that my father dressed well, in spite of limited funds and presented himself well to the public. My mother kept him in pressed shirts and one suit that she kept brushed and pressed for when he was out selling to the public. He was also impressed by my father's command of the English language.

Mr. Fulton also took note of his genuine interest in those with whom he came in contact and the congenial manner in which he greeted those newcomers who were struggling to communicate with the public in the new English language. Mike was always ready to learn a few words in their native tongue in order to make them feel more welcomed and would share with them the fact that he himself had been an immigrant only years earlier.

It was the right ingredients for a successful salesman. And Fulton did not find that my father's lack of a formal education was a deterrent factor when presenting himself to the public.

One day, he called Mike aside and asked him what he planned to do for his future. Had he any plans for feeding his growing family? My father knew something was on the banker's mind, but kept his expectations low along with his humility. Mr. Fulton made him aware that the Prudential Insurance Company was

The Other Marconi

opening new territories and he believed that my father was just the kind of individual they were looking for.

Mr. Fulton's keen observation of my father's communication skills had convinced him that he would be perfect for this new profession for which Prudential was seeking applicants. It was true that my father enjoyed speaking to people in their native tongue. He had already developed bits of conversation in Polish, Czech, Swedish, German and Russian.

"I'll bet that if you contact the local office of Prudential in Altoona they're going to find a job for you in one of their new mining territories. They need someone who can talk to the miners and let them know the value of having insurance. Your brother is a good example. Just think if he had had accident insurance at the time of that explosion," explained Fulton. Those words were relayed to me later when we would speak of his entry into the insurance field.

It made sense and so in 1926, Michael Albano began his twenty-eight year career with the Prudential Insurance Company. And he would tell his policy holders that he had passed that Rock of Gibraltar, (which was a symbol of the company's strength), when they were crossing the Atlantic from their home in Calabria.

The following year of 1927 the couple continued the growth of their family. It was May 5th this time, when a third daughter was born to Mike and Lucy and her name was a short version of my mother's full birth name: it was Mary Lou. The birth was a healthy delivery and showed no signs of any problems; they were happy to know that their third daughter was a healthy child. The fact that it was another girl, rather than the boy that Mike wanted so badly, did not prevent them from rejoicing. Now, each healthy child was seen as a blessing.

It is not certain what provisions were made to allow room for a third child, but there was either a room added to their present rental home or a move within Morrisdale that took place. Nevertheless, more living space was made to accommodate the family of five.

Now there was even more motivation for Mike to do well at his new job. And he was up to the challenge. He began to write more new policies and to show an increase in the size of the policies that were already on the books. His interest in his clients and their daily lives and desire to speak with them in their native tongues gained him both respect and trust as their insurance advisor.

In 1929 a fourth daughter was born to Mike and Lucy and she was named after relatives on both sides of the family: her name was Roseann. My father suggested Rose because they both had sisters named 'Rose' and Anna was the wife of a distant cousin (who would later become my godmother). Anna and Toby had become regular visitors and dinner guests of the prospering couple.

My mother had learned of the 'crush' on Rosina Catalano, who was now married to Mike Corina, however, and insisted that Mike had named their daughter to honor his first love's namesake. My father shrugged off such an accusation, truthfully acknowledging that they had never dated.

Of course the small home that they had rented as newlyweds had long outlived its usefulness. Once Mike established himself with Prudential, they moved to a larger house and began setting their sights on purchasing.

There were two events that finally led to the purchase of my parents' first home: the birth of the fourth daughter and the addition of a relative taking residence with our family. My mother's uncle Joe, seeking a place to live in the New World upon arriving from Italy, occurred shortly thereafter.

Chapter 23

In Common with Eddie Cantor

In 1932 my father found a commonality with the great comedian, Eddie Cantor. On March 22nd of that year, a fifth daughter was born to Mike and Lucy. This time my mother enjoyed the selection of her fifth daughter's name; she was named Joan. I was informed years later that her name had been inspired by the movie actress Joan Blondell. She had become a favorite of my mother's from her limited exposure to the silver screen.

My mother had also revealed her desire to have all five of her daughters schooled in tap or ballet, and she did realize that desire by the fact that each of my sisters had received lessons in at least one of those genres of the dance. And I am told that little Joan always had her hair curled in ringlets as though she was preparing to be a stand-in for the famed Shirley Temple.

My father accepted the idea of being the father of five daughters and compared his fortune to that of Eddie Cantor, also father of five girls.

Eddie Cantor was not the only star that Mike Albano was compared to, however; he had the solemn looks and high cheek bones that was sometimes identified with Clark Gable, and he seemed to draw the attention from the women that would have perhaps caused old Clark to consider him an off-stage rival!

My mother was fiercely jealous of my father and didn't trust him beyond the bedroom. But I felt sorry for my father when I would hear those stories because I once heard him swear on his mother's grave that he had never been unfaithful to my mother.

I found some of his writings later that would confirm such dedication and loyalty. I'm not sure that at that point in their marriage either of my parents had ever told the other all that they were feeling inside; it was very difficult for Old World Italians to express themselves to their spouses.

I did learn that my mother secretly admired the man whom she sometimes called a 'brute.' The term 'brute' in Italian had a slightly different meaning than that which was suggested from the English translation; it didn't mean someone who was unkind or bad, but to the Italian woman it was a man who was a flirt and being chased for his good looks—a man whose looks could make the girls cry with desire. That was a brute! Soon Mike would be tagged with a different name, that which was associated with the famous Italian inventor and a nickname which would remain with him for years to follow.

Relocation and Home Ownership

Just as one might argue about which came first, the chicken or the egg…I cannot be certain if it were immediately after or before the birth of my fifth sister, but it was definitely within that period of my parent's marriage that they purchased their first home. It was located in the small village of Munson, only a few miles from their former rentals in Morrisdale.

Great Uncle Joe, the brother of my maternal grandmother, had recently become widowed in Italy and desired to move close to family in America. His needs became the financial solution for my parents.

With the assistance of Uncle Joe, my parents were able to purchase the new home in Munson that was quite a good step up

The Other Marconi

from any previous residents. The house was located on several acres of ground. It had indoor plumbing and an enclosed front porch that would serve as my father's office. The grounds allowed ample space for gardening and it even provided space for a new interest for my mother: raising baby chicks.

It was during that same period of time, when Mike began to make himself useful around the house when small repairs had to be made. As a tenant, he had never shown any serious interest in fixing needed repairs, but now that he was a home owner he was determined to make things work and prove that he could be useful around the house.

The new home was one of the few houses in that small village that had a complete electric kitchen. Other homes had kitchens that depended on wood-burning or coal stoves for cooking. The new home also had complete indoor plumbing that included a modern bathroom.

Many of the homes still depended on outhouses rather than indoor toilets. However, all of our neighbors had indoor plumbing to the extent that they were not dependent on going to a well to draw water for consumption. But since indoor bathrooms were still a luxury, so was leisure bathing.

I still recall, as a child, walking in on my neighbors while the husband was taking his bath in the kitchen where a large tub held hot water that was heated on the coal stove.

I have chosen to insert this note at the end of the chapter because it was only a few months before going to press with this book that I learned of the obvious reversal of fortune that occurred within a relatively short time of my father's employment with Prudential—perhaps less than ten years. It was during a phone conversation with my sister Phyllis (who will turn 92 in just three months of this writing).

She explained the mystery of an in-ground swimming pool that I remembered at our Munson home. But by the time I was old enough to remember those details (about four years old), that pool was filled with various products of fill to prevent its use). According to my sister, the year would have been approximately 1936 when my sister was thirteen that my parents decided to have an in-ground pool built on the property, which contained several acres.

The swimming pool was constructed to provide my sisters with a private pool that would not be available to friends outside the family. Both of my parents feared diseases that could be carried within public pools; they were very protective of their children. In our conversation, my sister and I both agreed that we had grown up as privileged children without being cognizant of that fact.

In evaluating the events of that period of history, it would make sense that extra precautions were made because of the previous epidemics of cholera and diphtheria that had plagued many countries of Europe.

Chapter 24

The Naked Lady

By the time that my fifth sister was born, my father was comfortably established in his profession as an agent for the Prudential Insurance Company. He was well received into the homes of his clients and thought of as one of them: an Italian immigrant who understood the struggles of other families who had recently migrated to the New World and an individual who realized the importance of financial protection for the families of miners.

When he suggested new policies and additional coverage within existing policies they listened because they knew that he had seen the inside of a mine shaft and was able to relate to the concerns of those miners.

Mike had been with his company for almost ten years when Prudential began holding annual conventions in Atlantic City. It was the top producers that were encouraged to attend those conventions and my father was one of those top producers. His boss, in jest, suggested that he was a top producer on all fronts: he had fathered five daughters and…had expanded his insurance territory considerably.

I am told that my mother always had my father looking as sharp in his attire as he was in natural looks. I don't know if he had earned enough to purchase a second suit by that time, but the one suit that he had when he began with the company always looked fresh and there was always a fresh pressed and starched shirt and an attractive tie that complimented the pressed suit.

And so when he attended the conventions in Atlantic City it was surprising that upon his arrival at the hotel staff members often mistook him for the executive member of the company.

My sisters recalled that they looked forward to his return from the convention because he always brought them an ample supply of Salt Water Taffy.

There was one particular annual convention that I would like to share with my readers, however. It was a significant one!

The insurance conventions were unofficially referred to as "stag conventions." The justification was that there were no female insurance agents at the time and it didn't make sense for the agents to pay for their wives to attend a "working convention."

The expenses were paid for those agents who had met their quota of new policies during a designated period of time, and Mike always met or exceeded that quota.

Apparently one of the agents' wives overheard a conversation between her husband and a fellow agent stating how much fun this convention should be and that 'he wouldn't miss it for all the world!' She became curious as to how the convention could be so much fun when they were labeled as work conventions! So she decided to follow the convention to Atlantic City and surprise her husband! Her sister-in-law agreed to take her since she had her own car.

When the two women arrived at the hotel they inquired about the meeting rooms for the insurance convention. They were informed that there were private meetings being held during the luncheon and it was restricted to members only!

That only drew more interest and curiosity from the agent's wife. After placing her ear to the door of the banquet room and hearing some rather lurid commands being spoken by a female

The Other Marconi

voice…an erotic command that I shall refrain from writing in this story! The agent's wife bolted into the room to find that same female naked and seated comfortably on her husband's lap. He was the recipient of those sexual commands!

She charged directly to where her husband had pleasantly been seated and grabbed him by the neck, thereby escorting him out of the room.

The men were in shock! How could this have happened? The word got around to all of the agents' wives as to what sort of sales convention had taken place. That was the end of the stag conventions!

The wife of the supervising agent of my father's office declared that there would be no further conventions in Atlantic City unless she was going along as a paid guest; that would be the only circumstances by which she was going to approve of future conventions!

It was almost the end of the conventions, but the regional vice president found a compromising solution. I believe that he had some assistance in coming up with that solution. Hereafter, the wife of the regional manager or…a substitute wife would be invited to the convention at company's expense.

There was a fair amount of grumbling that went on among the agents as a result of that solution and some moaning by the husband whose wife made her grand entrance. He assured his fellow agents that he knew nothing about her plan and convinced his colleagues that he would have never informed her of their extracurricular activities. The agents knew that their conventions were never going to be the same.

The situation never presented itself where a substitute wife went in place of the regional vice president's wife, however. The alternate solution was to allow the regional secretary to attend; that was Mrs. Sally Palmer, a young grandmother of two small girls and…known to be a good 'Christian woman.'

Some of the wives didn't buy that solution, although it was true that Mrs. Palmer would not have sanctioned any 'extracurricular' activities. This alternative allowed for the men to still get away from their wives, but without any hanky-panky being sponsored by the company…at least where Mrs. Palmer was concerned. After all, the purpose of the company was to 'offer good policies!'

Mike assured Lucy that he had nothing to do with the entertainment and that it was the first convention where these shenanigans had taken place. That event stirred new distrust in the marriage and opened a wound from the pinching episodes.

After all future conventions, my father never failed to bring a gift home for my mother in addition to an abundance of salt water taffy for the family. At times my mother would bring up the infamous convention and suggest that my father was probably not in the corner playing Scrabble while the stripper was seated on the other agent's lap! That suggestive idea always brought an unnatural redness to his face!

Chapter 25

A New title for the Misses

Once the family moved to Munson to their new home, visitors became as frequent as customers going through the turnstile at Macy's. Now Mike and Lucy were able to welcome family members into their new, spacious home and often did so knowing that there would be the need for more settings at the kitchen table.

Everyone admired Lucy's cooking and it was a free night out for many of the wives who did not relish the idea of entertaining for large groups of relatives and/or friends. Of course it was natural for Italian families to welcome visitors to their dining table. Most of the agents were not of Italian decent and their wives were not accustomed to entertaining for dinners as was the normal Italian custom. So the parties continued to be a common and frequent ritual which concluded with dinner being served from Lucy's busy kitchen.

With Mike's growing success in the company and popularity among the other agents, it became common practice to have one or more of his agents and their spouses drop by for dinner… often unannounced to my mother. And this was in addition to many of the planned parties. After several months of non-stop dinner entertaining, my mother was bestowed the title of "Mrs. Prudential." And there were no agents' wives who wanted to compete for that title!

Soon, Mike would also earn a new title. It was not one that was given by family and friends, but rather by my mother. Once they had their own home, it seemed that there were always things to be fixed. Sometimes these were beyond my father's capacity to solve and sometimes he did manage to repair a fixture in his own inventive sort of way.

At times, my mother would become frustrated when the results caused more problems than solutions and would accuse my father of fixing things with chewing gum! But other times, as was the case with a clothesline and later with a pocket door leading to the bathroom, he came up with creative solutions.

And so my mother made a statement that stuck with my father for many years and repeated by many family and friends. She had been heard saying, "Yeah, you think you're Marconi!"

It was not realized at the time that my father did take serious the idea of inventing new and useful programs or ideas that could later benefit a society in progress.

There were times when my father did have success in repairing items and solving small problems and other times his efforts just compounded the problem. But when he was successful in finding ways to solve a problem, he looked for acknowledgment from my mother. Unfortunately he only heard the same remark, "Yeah, you think that you're Marconi!" It was often a left-handed compliment and other times a light compliment, but one to keep his pride in check.

As time progressed, several of the relatives and visiting friends became aware of the new title bestowed upon him by my mother and would ask, "And how is Marconi?"

Chapter 26

Marconi

In deference to the 'real Marconi,' I will take this opportunity to introduce the famous Italian inventor of the 19th Century.

Guglielmo Marconi, 1st Marquis of Marconi was born 25 April 1874, and died 20 July 1937. Marconi was an Italian inventor and electrical engineer, known for his pioneering work on long-distance radio transmission and for his development of Marconi's law and a radio telegraph system. He is often credited as the inventor of radio, and he shared the 1909 Nobel Prize in Physics with Karl Ferdinand Braun "in recognition of their contributions to the development of wireless telegraphy." He was an entrepreneur, businessman, and founder in Britain in 1897 of The Wireless Telegraph & Signal Company (which became the Marconi Company). Marconi succeeded in making a commercial success of radio by innovating and building on the work of previous experimenters and physicists. In 1929 the King of Italy ennobled Marconi as a Marchese (marquis).

Marconi was born into the Italian nobility as Guglielmo Giovanni Maria Marconi in Bologna, the second son of Giuseppe Marconi (an Italian aristocratic landowner from Porretta Terme) and of his Irish/Scots wife, Annie Jameson. Between the ages of two and six Marconi, along with his elder brother Alfonso, was brought up by his mother in the English town of Bedford. After returning to Italy he received his early education privately in Bologna in the lab of Augusto Righi, in Florence at the Istituto

Cavallero and, later, in Livorno. As a child, according to Robert McHenry, Marconi did not do well in school, though historian Corradi Giuliano in his biography characterizes him as a true genius.

During his early years, Marconi had an interest in science and electricity. One of the scientific developments during this era came from Heinrich Hertz, who, beginning in 1888, demonstrated that one could produce and detect electromagnetic radiation—now generally known as radio waves, at the time more commonly called "Hertzian waves" or "aetheric waves". Hertz's death in 1894 brought published reviews of his earlier discoveries, and a renewed interest on the part of Marconi. He was permitted to briefly study the subject under Augusto Righi, a University of Bologna physicist and neighbor of Marconi who had done research on Hertz's work.

Marconi began to conduct experiments, building much of his own equipment in the attic of his home at the Villa Griffone in Pontecchio, Italy, with the help of his butler Mignani. His goal was to use radio waves to create a practical system of "wireless telegraphy"—i.e. the transmission of telegraph messages without connecting wires as used by the electric telegraph. This was not a new idea—numerous investigators had been exploring wireless telegraph technologies for over 50 years, but none had proven technically and commercially successful.

One night in December, Guglielmo woke his mother up and invited her into his secret workshop and showed her the experiment he had created. The next day he also showed his work to his father, who, when he was certain there were no wires, gave his son all of the money he had in his wallet so Guglielmo could buy more materials.

In the summer of 1895 Marconi moved his experimentation outdoors and continued to experiment on his father's estate in Bologna. After increasing the length of the transmitter and

The Other Marconi

receiver antennas, arranging them vertically, and positioning the antenna so that it touched the ground, the range increased significantly. Soon he was able to transmit signals over a hill, a distance of approximately 2.4 kilometres (1.5 mi).[19] By this point he concluded that with additional funding and research, a device could become capable of spanning greater distances and would prove valuable both commercially and militarily.

Marconi wrote to the Ministry of Post and Telegraphs, then under the direction of the honorable Pietro Lacava, explaining his wireless telegraph machine and asking for funding. He never received a response to his letter which was eventually dismissed by the Minister who wrote "to the Longara" on the document, referring to the insane asylum on Via della Lungara in Rome.

In 1896, Marconi spoke with his family friend Carlo Gardini, Honorary Consul at the United States Consulate in Bologna, about leaving Italy to go to England. Gardini wrote a letter of introduction to the Ambassador of Italy in London, Annibale Ferrero, explaining who Marconi was and about these extraordinary discoveries. In his response, Ambassador Ferrero advised them not to reveal the results until after they had obtained the copyrights. He also encouraged him to come to England where he believed it would be easier to find the necessary funds to convert the findings from Marconi's experiment into a practical use. Finding little interest or appreciation for his work in Italy, Marconi traveled to London in early 1896 at the age of 21, accompanied by his mother, to seek support for his work; Marconi spoke fluent English in addition to Italian. Marconi arrived at Dover and at Customs the Customs officer opened his case to find various contraptions and apparatus. The customs officer immediately contacted the Admiralty in London. While there, Marconi gained the interest and support of William Preece, the Chief Electrical Engineer of the British Post Office.

"…by March 1897, Marconi had transmitted Morse code signals over a distance of about 6 kilometres (3.7 mi) across Salisbury Plain. On 13 May 1897, Marconi sent the world's first ever wireless communication over open sea. The experiment, based in Wales, witnessed a message transversed over the Bristol Channel from Flat Holm Island to Lavernock Point in Penarth, a distance of 6 kilometres (3.7 mi)…." For more on Guglielmo Marconi, one can find the complete history and background of this famous 'real Marconi' by going to Google and then seeking the 'complete story.'

It is not difficult to understand how this Italian-born genius would influence his fellow-Italians and become a household word, even when comparing him favorably to a husband whose ideas did not measure that of a genius. The mere mention of Marconi in the same sentence as one's spouse could be considered a compliment… albeit often a left-handed compliment!

Note: *Much of the information obtained for this chapter was a result of consulting Google online.*

Chapter 27

Naughty Marconi

It was the 'naughty' episodes that drove my parents to separate bedrooms shortly after my sister Joan was born. The family grew in age, although not in size, and my parents began to resume their social activities of entertaining and attending family outings that were hosted by some of the many cousins and cousins of cousins.

In those days, a distant cousin was still regarded as a *cugino* or *cugina*. And that relative deserved the respect of children. There were many older cousins who were regarded as uncles and aunts; they were addressed as such rather than as Mr. or Mrs. by the children of the Italian families, and never by just a first name.

It was probably one of the second or third cousins who had a hunting lodge where many parties were held. The Italian men were not known to be hunters of wild game such as deer or turkey, but some did enjoy the luxury of owning a 'hunting cabin' where family gatherings and special parties were held.

According to stories told to me by my mother, the year must have been 1937 or early 1938 when they attended a party at the cousin's hunting cabin. My mother was not very interested in attending these parties, but she knew that Mike wanted to go so she decided that she would please him by going. It was usually not a good idea to turn down an invitation by another Italian family; feelings were easily hurt.

After about an hour of attending the party, Lucy discovered that Mike was nowhere in sight…shall we say AWOL! She began asking some of the guests if they had seen him, but were only told that perhaps he had gone outdoors to explore the grounds. My mother knew that my father was never especially fond of walking in the woods so she began to look within the lodge for him.

One of the cousins who was still single had brought a very attractive young woman to the party with him and she had gained the attention of many of the men. She was dressed more appropriately for a night out on the town than a country picnic. Her low-cut blouse left nothing to the imagination!

Lucy noticed one door at the end of the hall closed. She decided to take a stroll in that direction and heard sounds from within. She put her ear closer to the door and heard the woman say, "I hear that you like to do some pinching. How would you like to pinch these?" She heard Mike respond by saying, "I really should get back to the party." With that, she opened the door and found Mike glaring at the almost-naked breasts that was cleverly held by a low-cut top. Needless to say, the party was over!

I'm told that at first there were tears of hurt by my mother. But when that didn't seem to put an end to the nasty habit and she was not convinced of sincere remorse, she resorted to the old cure that she and her sister-in-law had been successful with a few years earlier…although they were warned that it was a dangerous method of punishment that could lead their husbands to stray from their matrimonial duties!

Lucy wasn't worried about that happening; she did believe her husband to be faithful but to weaken when it came to touching the merchandise, so she put her foot down and the bedroom door was locked for several weeks…perhaps months after the hunting lodge episode.

As an adult son, a more detailed version of that story was shared with me; I was told that she had read the riot act to him saying, "…there won't be any son because there won't be any more children if you aren't sleeping in my bed!" That was the bitter medicine that stopped the pinching—both behind and in front!

I'm told that my mother used her method of punishment anytime that she thought my father was too frisky with female guests…even if the flirtations were initiated by the female. He learned to excuse himself from temptations because he didn't enjoy the consequences that resulted by doing otherwise.

Having more children became a remote possibility as the early years passed after the birth of their fifth daughter, although being Catholic and following the rules and practices of the church made it difficult to turn off the pregnancy wheel for many of those Catholic families.

Perhaps the legitimate problem of my father being a loud snorer helped to justify separate bedrooms for the couple. Now any late night rendezvous would have to be conducted quietly and after all the children had fallen asleep. The new normal served a dual purpose because it contributed to a quiet night's sleep and somewhat of a natural practice for birth control.

Couples who chose separate bedrooms no longer had to deal with difficult confessions at the 'confession box!' Eventually, my parents resumed their normal matrimonial activities behind closed doors, but the brassiere incident never left my mother's mind, and when she needed some ammunition to keep him in check she reminded him of it.

Chapter 28
An Unexpected Arrival

Somehow, after seven years of my father often 'being in the desert,' due to his penchant for pinching, my mother found herself pregnant once again in 1938. It was an unexpected visit from the stork…although these visits were always welcomed, albeit the seven years since the stork's last visit. I think my parents thought that that bird was destined for other homes now.

At the time of discovery, as the story was told, my mother was attending the ordination of a priest who was a distant cousin. She had accepted the church invitation from a cousin who was so proud to honor her brother by attending his ordination. My parents both had a profound respect for the church and thought it an honor that my mother was an invited guest.

It was during the actual ceremony that she became somewhat ill. She looked back at what she had eaten that day, but the truth was that she had hardly eaten before attending the ceremony and yet she felt nauseated. Her first suspicion was that perhaps she should have eaten something of substance before leaving for the ceremony. But then she began to think that this uncomfortable feeling had visited her six times before! Upon returning home and checking her 'schedule,' she wondered if it were possible that after seven years she could be pregnant again.

I was born on March 14, 1939. My father had his son! And the celebration went from one week to the next…at least it seemed that way for those years later who recalled the celebration. My mother wanted me to carry the name of my father, but they had already named their first son Michael and my father had his own idea as to whose name I should bear.

Eugenio Pacelli had been elevated to Pope Pius XII earlier that same month; his papacy began on March 2nd. My father had the idea that he owed a special thanks to God for bringing him his son. My parents compromised and I was named Eugenio Michael Albano.

My father had been with Prudential for thirteen years at that point in time and they also threw him a party to celebrate the birth of his son. His fellow agents had known for some time that Mike yearned for a son.

On the last day of August in 1941, a second surprise package arrived at the Albano residence; it would be the final visit by the stork—a second son who was named Michael Angelo (respecting the name of Lucy's brother, Angelo) and not repeating the exact name of the first born son. Now my mother had her way in giving this son my father's surname and now the family was complete. Even my mother was calling for time out. Basta, basta cosi!

Now Mike proudly touted his 'two sons.' It was not uncommon for him to refer to his sons with great pride as his two boys…as though they were the entire family! But most of the girls were old enough to enjoy, rather than resent, these new surprise arrivals. After all, there were eighteen years difference between the oldest daughter, Elizabeth, and son Michael. And of course sixteen years between her and yours truly.

This span of age had its rewards for Lucy because now she could put her oldest daughters: Elizabeth and Filomena (quickly known to the family as Betty and Phyllis), in charge when she needed some freedom for a bit of independence.

The constant entertaining with impromptu dinners were decreased considerably, although the cousins still enjoyed dropping

Eugenio Michael Albano

in unannounced. But now some of the closer family members would bring something with them…even if it were small items to go with my mother's spaghetti dishes—perhaps Italian black olives or a bottle of wine.

Lucy had not only gained a reputation for her spaghetti and meatballs, but my siblings and I recall the smell of fresh baked bread coming out of the oven and garnished with olive oil and oregano. It was the only bread that I ever craved.

Mike Albano was more enthused about inviting friends and family members to the house than ever before; he wanted the world to share in his joy of having sons. My brother's birth was more demanding on my mother than with my arrival because she returned to breast-feeding, whereas I had to have a manufactured formula due to allergies.

It seemed that my mother always had the pot boiling for that next serving of spaghetti for last minute dinner guests. But now she had valued assistance from her grown daughters. Each one of them took pleasure in doting over their baby brothers. So the duties of "Mrs. Prudential" continued and Mike Albano was happy that he had his family of five girls and two boys. He finally had his sons!

I am told that my father spent fewer hours away from home after my brother and I were 'in the picture.' Both of his parents had passed on and he looked forward to spending time with his sons. He managed to avoid evening appointments that were usually required to discuss new policies with the mining husband. Perhaps he would leave the necessary information and papers with the wife…or maybe he called back on a rare Saturday visit. But his evenings were spent enjoying his sons before their bedtime.

From time to time, Lucy was still warned by her sister-in-law, who no longer lived in Pennsylvania, "…to keep an eye on Mike!" She told my mother that even with Roy's peg leg, she wouldn't trust him past the drug store! These brothers had rightfully earned the reputation as Romeos and they were 'shamefully handsome men.'

It was often not their doing that the women continued swooning over them, knowing full well that they were not available. The wives did everything but post signs on their husbands that the men were "off limits."

It should be noted that the in-ground swimming pool that had been built only three years earlier for my five sisters was completely filled shortly after I began to walk. My father was taking no chances that I could wander down to the pool site and fall in. So the once-enjoyed pool was now filled with ashes and other suitable debris that would not allow its use anymore.

Chapter 29

Distance...and the Hearts Grow Fonder

After the years when the families of brothers Mike and Roy expanded and children were growing into young adults, a move caused the brothers to be separated. But distance never weakened the bonding that these two brothers held close all of their lives.

Roy's family was growing in age and like his sisters who had re-located to New Jersey, his older children had sought better employment opportunities and he, himself, found little future in the clerical position held at the local post office. So Roy's family eventually moved to Linden, New Jersey where other family members had settled.

When the brothers got together, several times each year, there were always stories to share between them. The pinching had to be retired in order for the families to survive and grow, but Roy always enjoyed the latest stories that were told to him about the activities of the insurance group of men.

It was still a man's world when it came to employment and so that aside from the secretaries, Prudential had maintained an all-male sales force. It's amazing, however, how women can learn to hold power over the men who enjoy a heaping portion of late thirties/early forties testosterone. Sometimes the wives found great satisfaction in communicating, and the telephone began to serve as a household item rather than a luxury during that time. Although there were few, if any, books written about 'how to keep your husband in check,' the telephone allowed the wives to share ideas

The Other Marconi

about how to do just that—although phone calls were kept short since, at that time in our history, the telephone was considered an instrument designed for calls of necessity and/or emergency calls; toll calls were even considered from one nearby town to the other!

My father did not get out to the Jersey side too often because of his work schedule, but Roy had a much better situation…perhaps not as good a paying one, but certainly a more flexible time-off schedule. And when Mike's brother and his wife were coming to Philipsburg, it was practically a declared holiday that involved the Catalanos, the Albertos, the Albanos, and…a newer clan known as the Prestipinos. Somehow that last clan entered the scene later as cousins were marrying into new Italian families.

When the two brothers did get together, Nervie and Lucy would accept the fact that for the next few days it was going to be them for themselves. Of course there was always much to discuss: the Albertos had nine children and the Albano family was now a family of seven. The baby race and the counting stopped after the birth of my brother Michael.

Chapter 30

New Friends, New Interests

It was the early 1940's and our nation was involved in a war. Suddenly, many Americans who had not previously been concerned about our nation's news became glued to the radio to learn of the latest developments of that war—known as World War II. It was during that same time that a new couple entered my parents' lives: Tom and Blanche Sinclair.

Tom Sinclair was involved in labor relations with the railroad and Blanche held a position with the county Democrats. The couple had no children and Blanche was one of few women at the time who had her own car; she was the personification of the liberated woman. Women's Liberation had not yet found its name in society, but Blanche would have been considered a trailblazer!

My father became fascinated by her knowledge of politics and began to take a real interest in politics in the news. Tom was a quiet man but displayed considerable knowledge and authority in the discussion of labor relations. The couple took a genuine liking to my parents and Blanche became my mother's great cheerleader for independence.

Blanche told my mother that she should get out more since her oldest daughters were certainly capable of looking after the youngest in the family. She would scold Mike for keeping my mother tied to the house, perhaps replacing the phrase 'barefoot and pregnant!' *She was seldom barefoot, but she had been too often pregnant—according to Blanche.* Of course the only real reason

The Other Marconi

that most women were 'tied to the house' in those days was due to the fact that few families owned more than one automobile.

Mike discovered two genres of broadcasting that earned his loyalty to the radio: world news and opera. I cannot be certain how he learned so much about opera in such a relatively short period of time, but I do recall his vast knowledge of Italian operas: the composers and the many arias.

By early 1943, while my brother was barely two years old and I was approaching four, Blanche Sinclair had become a true mentor for my mother. She was taxiing her into town to shop and encouraged my mother to start charging money for items that she had sewn or knitted for others beyond the needs of her own children. Lucy was learning how to be a business woman if it only meant that she could now contribute a small amount towards her grocery expenses for the kitchen.

Blanche would scold my mother and advise her to hold onto that extra money. "Lucy," she would snap, "your husband is making enough to support the family and provide for household needs. You put that sewing money in a little jar for your own personal needs!" That advice was later told to me by Blanche, herself. And, I must say…Blanche made me aware just how spoiled I was by my father. "Hershey bars as a child when chocolate was very expensive during wartime," she told me. "But nothing was too good for little Genie," she would repeat.

Yes, that was my childhood name by the family—not Eugenio or Eugene or even Gene—it was "little Genie." (Truth be told…I was a rather chubby little boy)! I can still hear Blanche, with her somewhat rough, coughing voice… due to her heavy cigarette smoking…,"You were spoiled rotten!" But then she would embellish her assessment by telling me that I was a good boy, "just awfully spoiled," she would add.

My father would sometimes share his new ideas with Tom Sinclair and Tom would advise him to get those ideas to the US Patent Office before somebody else got credit for them.

Mike was sensing a new streak of independence in his wife, but he found himself pleased rather than remorseful. He discovered that he liked this new assertive woman that Blanche Sinclair had brought out in her. He was confident that she would never become the dominant woman that his dear mother had become late in her marriage, but he would have never wanted a submissive wife that mirrored her own mother.

Nevertheless, at this stage of their marriage, Mrs. Prudential was still commonly referred to as "Mike's wife" among his policy holders. Most of his clients had never met her, and they hadn't bothered to know her name, but they knew him well and they knew that he had a wife and family, so she was just known to them as 'Mike's wife'!

Chapter 31
Independence Day

By 1943 the family at home had decreased. Both Betty and Phyllis, now nineteen and twenty were well situated in their careers in Philadelphia. Betty had entered the Rudemar Beauty School shortly after high school and Phyllis had decided that she wanted to follow in her older sister's footsteps.

Mary Lou, was now sixteen and old enough to look after the younger members of the family. Roseann was fourteen and did not need much supervision, so between the two sisters they provided the supervision for their two small brothers and the youngest sister who was eleven. They had also assumed some of the responsibilities of household chores.

By that time, Lucy had two mentors who provided her with transportation and business ideas. Rose Corina (who now became known as Rosie) had also become a close friend. Like Blanche Sinclair, she also had the luxury of having her own car and would often come to visit and offer my mother a ride into town to shop and to observe life outside of the family. It became known that Rose's family, the Catalanos, was distant cousins of Lucy's mother. This discovery gave both women an added incentive to get to know each other. Between these two women, Lucy was, in a sense, becoming more liberated as well. Suddenly 'Mrs. Prudential' was experiencing a freedom and independence that no one could have foreseen.

Blanche not only encouraged my mother to get out more often, but she began telling my mother that she should stop cooking for the whole relationship. Once, I heard her repeat what she had years earlier told my mother, "God, Lucy, when do you get to be on the receiving side? Don't you realize that you'll have these folks coming to your house forever as long as there are free meals and the wives don't have to mess up their kitchens?"

It was during that time in their marriage (circa 1944) that a weekend drive in the country led to an entirely new independence for my mother and opened a new chapter in the lives of Mike and his "Bashful Lucy!"

It was never known which of the two women, Blanche or Rose had more to do with introducing Lucy to the idea of "women's liberation," but my mother found it before it was a common word in the household dictionary. *I suspect that it might have been Blanche!*

Although Blanche and Rosie had exposed my mother to more freedom through constantly providing her with transportation away from the house, neither woman had thought of acting on their independence in the manner in which my mother would soon advance. However, both of these women played an active role in transforming Mike's 'bashful Lucy' from housewife to businesswoman and later entrepreneur—perhaps introducing society to **women's liberation!**

It was in the spring of 1944 and several months before little Michael would celebrate his third birthday that Mike and Lucy decided to take a ride through the countryside. We already lived 'in the country,' but to drive through the small towns and villages and pass creeks and small clumps of forests were a couple's primary way of enjoying a weekend. There were no planned vacations for this class of society: those who were struggling…comfortably or uncomfortably to meet the basic needs of the family.

The Other Marconi

To this day, it has never been revealed—and now with their passing it never will be, what prompted my parents to take that 'ride in the country.' Was it a scheme orchestrated by my mother, or was it just happenstance? Either way, my mother spotted a yard sale at one of the homes along that country road.

Perhaps it was a sale that had been organized by several neighbors because there were some items that were being sold in numbers. There were three wind-up Victrolas being offered...and they were cheap! There were some lamps, tables and chairs and a bedroom chest of drawers.

Of course today the Victrola would be an antique dealer's dream, but then society was preparing for the new electric box that served the same purpose, (except that the new electric Victrola required a separate amplifier to hear the recording).

The disposing of the old 'wind-up' Victrola might be compared to today's disposal of an antiquated mobile phone in order to enjoy the features of the newer phone and subsequently the Smartphone.

I was only five at the time, but I still recall those old phonographs in her store with the logo of "His Masters Voice" depicting the dog looking into an Edison Bell cylinder.

For about 50 cents each, Lucy bought all three of those music boxes. She also snapped up the lamps and the table and chairs. Mike was utterly amazed at this turn of events. First of all, he didn't know that his wife had any money of her own, so his question had been, "Why stop when we have no money to spare?" And secondly, he had no idea why she would be interested in this 'old junk' that was being disposed of.

Well, the answers were quick in coming. She had managed to save up seven dollars from extra items of children's clothing she had made on request by neighbors and relatives. Her reputation as the seamstress of all of her daughters beautiful dresses had gone public!

The big surprise came when she informed her husband that she knew of an empty barn in Winburne, just a few miles from their home in Munson. She continued to explain that upon inquiring she had learned that the barn had never been used for animals but had only stored farm equipment and was available.

Lucy wanted to start a small furniture store! My father was absolutely taken aback! When had all of this entered her mind? Why hadn't he heard about this earlier? But Mike knew that when his wife decided to do something, it was happening!

There were many questions that 'the other Marconi' would ask and…she had answers for them all!

More can be learned about this 'wonder woman' in the biographical novel, "Bashful Lucy."

Chapter 32
Farewell to Mrs. Prudential

It was obvious that the woman who had entertained her husband's fellow agents and their wives and the entire Italian clan and had kept her house clean and all seven children well-fed and ready for public scrutiny (including the youngest of those girls coiffed with long ringlets) was going to have to give up something in order to become the new operator of a furniture store. And so the grand dinner parties came to a halt. Obviously, the care for the children could not…and would not. But that part of the duties did receive some valuable assistance from the eldest of three remaining daughters at home.

My father continued to enjoy his young family and began focusing on the several inventive ideas that might lead to a worthwhile patent. It was during that period of time that I believe he worked on some sort of expandable clothesline (perhaps an improved motorized line that had already been invented or…in process of being patented) and other household ideas.

From my recollection, I don't believe the highway track and bank robber trap doors entered my father's mind until the early years of the following decade.

Chapter 33

New Roles - New Identities

So now Michael and Lucy Albano had carved out their own separate niches in the community. Among my father's policy holders the couple was known only as Mike Albano and Mike's wife. But now, in the local business community the couple would become known as Lucy Albano and Lucy's husband…! The opening of a furniture store became only the stepping stone for "Marconi's" wife.

As my mother became successful in sales of furniture she also learned about property…especially property that was being repossessed by the local bank in Philipsburg. Her story is already written in my previous biographical novel, "Bashful Lucy."

As stated at the beginning of this chapter, my parents had carved out their own individual niche in society. And yet, when they were among their friends and relatives they were Mike and Lucy. My father showed no interest in becoming involved in my mother's business ventures which began with the furniture store but eventually expanded to property investments and management of rental properties. And my mother never had even a curious interest in learning about life insurance or any of the various programs associated with the insurance business.

Mike did continue going to the Atlantic City conventions but now there was at least one of the wives who went along. If the boss's wife was unavailable to attend, then Mrs. Palmer attended.

And to be sure…there were no more strip shows! However, the practice of bringing back salt water taffy for the family and a souvenir from the boardwalk for my mother continued.

In 1945 the family had moved to Philipsburg where they could provide more opportunities for the teenage daughters and where Lucy also relocated her furniture store. When asked about the various properties that were being purchased, my father would concede that he only went along to the bank to sign papers. He never felt the need to take credit away from his *Bashful Lucy*.

Mary Lou was graduating from high school and Roseann had quit school to help take care of my brother and me. She had been protesting school for several years and had convinced my parents that she could serve the family better by being home and helping my mother to further her business ambitions. She had no interest in high school studies and had been looking for an excuse to quit school.

In 1946 my father received his first major recognition from the Prudential Insurance Company for his outstanding performance as their agent. He was presented with a gold pocket watch fab that could also serve as a locket. It was made of 18k gold and had on its cover a bas relief of a seal with a ruby in its eye and a small diamond on the belly. My father wore that fab on his pocket watch chain for several months and then decided that it should be placed in a safe box for future consideration.

He had wanted to put my mother's picture in one of the two places inside the locket but wasn't sure how to deal with the remaining space since there were two sons to consider. My mother solved the problem for him by suggesting that both sons' photos should go inside and some day she would have the pleasure of wearing the locket.

Mr. McGraw, the regional vice president from Altoona, reminded Mike that upon twenty-five years of service the company would want the locket back…to replace the diamond with a slightly larger one. Mike indicated that he would look forward to that day because he had no plans to leave the company. Undoubtedly, this was the company's clever method of holding on to their top agents.

Chapter 34
Monopoly Played Once Again

By 1948 many new events saw "Marconi" and "Bashful Lucy" making more progress. Lucy decided that the family should move to a larger, more luxurious home…although Mike was quite content with the present one. But Lucy had grandiose ideas for the type of home 'her' daughters should be married from! At that time in the family's history four of the five daughters had not yet married. And so, they moved from Fifth Street to Seventh Street to a property known to many in the town as 'the little white house' because of its prominent façade and commanding elevation on the large corner lot.

Mary Lou was now dating a childhood crush who had recently returned from the Navy. His family, who resided in Bellefonte, was quite successful in business ventures and my future brother-in-law had one day showed up sporting a new deluxe Chevrolet. 'Marconi' got the idea that he should have new wheels since he was enjoying some success in sales and recognition by his company. So…without consultation, one Saturday he announced that he would be going to a garage to have the oil changed. Later that afternoon…many hours later… he returned with a new 1948 maroon Chevrolet.

There had been no discussion about purchasing a new car, but when he was confronted by my mother…he reminded her that he had never interfered with her decisions to purchase properties, so he assumed that he should have the same right to purchase a new automobile. This was just another example of the individualism that each one enjoyed…sometimes at the consternation of the other!

Other significant events occurred for Mike and Lucy that same year. The youngest daughter in the family who had been permitted to accept an engagement ring from her soldier boyfriend decided to marry that same year.

The wedding was cleverly planned between two sisters and the couple eloped. Within days of the elopement, the couple were marched to the chapel of the local Catholic Church and were married by the local priest. Now all concerned were happy and we all welcomed the young veteran into our family. I might add that he had already won favor with my mother.

More weddings would soon follow and in each of those weddings Mike proudly walked his daughters down the aisle after Lucy had overseen the production of the weddings.

The Inventor

During this time in my father's life, he continued developing new ideas to submit to the US Patent Office. At the same time his passion for opera continued to grow.

Tom and Blanche Sinclair continued to be close friends of my parents and as I was approaching my teens they would enjoy recalling the early years of their friendship with Mike and Lucy. My father found Tom to be an excellent sounding board in which to share his latest ideas and possible inventions.

Some of those ideas that had been submitted to the US Patent Office are mentioned below:

The Bank Trap

When I was in my teens my father had begun drawing plans for catching bank robbers by installing trap-door devices on the floor of the banks in front of each teller's window. The teller would simply press a button at her station and before the thief could react, he would find himself in the basement of the bank and within a metal cage. *Of course the invention included a padded landing so that the bank would not be the subject of a lawsuit for major injuries.*

I think 'Marconi' got his idea from the magicians who made themselves disappear through a trap-door (but of course the black cloak was supposed to be responsible for their disappearance). When confronted with the expense that would be required to build these contraptions, my father argued that it would be worth it to save the banking institutions the cost of recovering millions of lost funds.

I still recall the elaborate drawings that he had made to submit to the bureau of patents. I think he did get a reply, but it wasn't an encouraging one. I suppose most of the replies from the patent office were similar to those received by authors like myself: "Thank you for your submission, but at this time we are not accepting unsolicited manuscripts." When you receive enough of those letters, you can recite the letter verbatim!

The Great Road Plan

Another of the creative ideas that my father shared with me was a new idea in long distance transportation that he felt would reduce highway accidents and eliminate congestion as well. He never did like to drive in cities and seldom experienced highway traffic because his day-to-day work kept him on country roads… some even being unpaved ones.

His idea was that someday cars would all be on tracks and the track would take them to a pre-determined destination. He explained that once you drove your car out of the driveway, you would drive to a station where the car would be put on a track… much the same as a trolley.

He explained that the driver would have a choice of several destinations, for example: if you were planning to go to the city of Philadelphia, you would choose that track and pay a toll in advance. If you were going to Chicago or New York City you would have your car placed on that track.

It's possible that my father got his idea from the newly constructed Pennsylvania Turnpike, although my father insisted that his idea was a unique and different concept. And he added that with his invention of tracks, once on the track you would have to go to that destination. There would be gas pumps along the way, but you could not get off the track

When my mother heard him repeating this concept to me, she called in from the kitchen and told him that she wished that years ago he had invented a track that would have brought him directly home from the office on payday, rather than stopping off to make grocery purchases that neither suited her list of items needed for the week, nor worked into the budget she had developed for that week's groceries.

Anytime that my mother came up with such an affront Mike would grow silent and walk away humming or whistling some aria from a favorite opera. It was his way of kindly blowing off her retort. It made for a comical One Act!

They seldom got angry over these little jabs at each other. More often than not, it was their way of entertaining each other with an amusing bit of conversation. It was times like this that, as I grew older, I would affectionately refer to them as the real life "Maggie and Jiggs."

While most of my parents' friends referred to them as Mike and Lucy, there were a few close friends and family members who would still occasionally ask, "How is Marconi these days?" I'm sure this light-spirited comment came as a result of hearing my mother joke about her inventive husband who thought he was Marconi.

The Other Marconi

I had often heard my mother say, "Yeah, you think you're Marconi!" But sometimes it was not as left-handed a compliment as it was a 'flirtatious jab.' My mother did not approve of openly flirtatious behavior in public. Au contraire! It was usually my father wanting to flirt, but my mother would have none of it in the presence of their children.

There were other creative ideas in which my father had great hopes for acceptance, but none ever came to fruition. I do recall that he went to great lengths to have his trap door for bank thieves accepted. He had professional drawings made up by a registered draftsman and would proudly show those plans which he had submitted to the US Office of Patents to visiting guests.

Chapter 35

Compassion Has Its Price

The issues that followed the earlier days of 'Marconi' playing Romeo to a wrong Juliet was not the only bone of contention in the Albano household. There were times that my father would come home from his Friday payday short of the amount noted on his pay statement. My mother wanted an explanation for the shortage. It was not always due to a stop-off at the grocery store. Where had the difference in the paycheck gone?

My father was not a 'drinker' so he hadn't stopped at some local bar on the way. No, it was a different sort of illegal activity that could have possibly gotten my father fired at the time!

There was no shortage of compassion by either of my parents, but in this case it was my father's concern for the families of miners who were his policy holders. My father was aware of the importance of miners' families being protected in the event of a mining accident that could either cause permanent injury or even death that would result in a lasting hardship to the family. At that time in our country's history very few wives worked outside of the home. Families depended on the miner's income to sustain the family and provide any future for their children.

It was against company policy to pay for a policy holder's premium. But Mike knew the importance of not allowing his customers' policies to lapse so he occasionally paid the premium out of his own pocket and would accept produce from the family garden as payment in kind.

He did his best to avoid this conversation from being played out because he had memorized the results: "Oh, so you are taking care of someone else's problems! Well, who is supposed to feed your family?" However, Mike was confident that his wife could manage with her keen sense of budgeting. And he would argue that the produce that he had accepted would help to replace the funds that would have purchased similar items from the grocery store. It was a frequent bone of contention that gave food to a weekend argument.

My father seldom argued, however. He would state his case and then merely walk away. He had a genuine compassion for the people with whom he became acquainted within his policy route (or debit as it had been called). His 'big heart' caused ongoing debate and differences within the marriage, however.

Mike could never be accused of being a dominating partner, but neither was he a husband who had ever gotten used to handing over a paycheck to his wife.

Years later in their marriage, the inventive Marconi found an example of his wife's flawed practice in business that also caused her to shortchange her own sales income.

It was several years later, but Mike had not forgotten the coals he had walked over for paying small premiums from his own earnings in order to keep policies in force when a family couldn't afford to do so.

We may leap forward over a few years of events, but I believe this is the proper time to reveal that flaw in my mother's dealings of retail business. It was a compassionate practice that paralleled my father's generosity to his policy holders. And Mike was feeling quite self-congratulatory for finally finding a parallel to the issue that caused many unnecessary arguments in the home. *One might consider it an inventive volley!*

I had also witnessed these "random acts of kindness" when occasionally stopping by the store.

The store was now located on Front Street in Philipsburg and age had mellowed both of my parents. My father was in the background while my mother was showing some new table and chairs to a young, newly married couple who were just beginning to go housekeeping. The young man had just begun new employment and they had no credit standing and very little cash.

The breakfast set was probably priced at about $135. When they were shown the lovely new set, the couple quickly stated that the price was 'way beyond their means.' They needed to look at something that they could afford.

My mother never sold 'junk' but she also never wanted to sell an item that wasn't practical for the purchaser. She knew that this couple could not afford the set, but she also knew that if they went elsewhere they might settle for a rickety old table and chairs that would soon need to be replaced; in the final analysis it would be more costly for them. She wanted them to have what their hearts desired.

They admitted that they liked the set, but it was beyond what they could afford. Lucy quickly interrupted the wife's apologetic response informing the couple that it was 'on sale' and she had just not gotten around to changing the price. "I could let you have it for $100," she inserted. "And I will extend a line of credit for you as long as I have your word that I can count on your payments." She offered these terms without having done a credit check or verifying the man's employment.

My father knew of no sale beginning and he knew that my mother often lost money when customers did not honor their credit accounts. In fact, she had probably paid $100 for the set because she never marked up her items beyond a modest small profit.

When the couple left the store…with the new kitchen set being loaded to their pick-up truck, my father decided that this was an opportune time to remind her of the many times that she had confronted him on his Friday payday. He reminded my mother of her lectures about paying policy premiums (which were substantially less money…perhaps $2 or $3 premiums). And it was one of few times when my mother had no response.

It had taken considerable years to do so, but now my father… the creative Marconi had finally cancelled out the issue that had dogged him for years.

The truth of the matter was that both of my parents were very compassionate individuals in their separate ways. But their 'random acts of kindness' had shown through at different stages of their lives and now the 'Santa Claus' lady who was willing to 'give away the store' had finally been challenged by the inventive husband who she had labeled as attempting to be Marconi!

Chapter 36

Becoming of Age---Asking the Question

When I was still living at home and in high school I recalled finding my mother in the kitchen rolling dough. I thought it was the perfect time to ask her a question that had been on my mind, and I felt confident that under these circumstances the question would not offend her because she was focusing on her project with hands busy in the dough.

I asked her why she was so hard on 'Marconi' as far as holding back compliments and assurance. She responded without hesitation. She asked me if I ever watched a rooster in the hens' house, prancing around like a big shot.

I was a bit taken aback…I hardly remembered that hen house in Munson since we moved before I turned six. And I hadn't immediately seen how my question could be related to that hen house! However, I could imagine the picture that she was painting for me, so I told her that I did recall that scene…but how did that relate to my father's behavior? "Well," she said…with great focus on her dough rolling. "Have you ever seen a photo of your father as a young man…in his late teens or even our wedding picture?" I realized that I had not seen the photos to which she was referring; they were never displayed. And since I was the sixth child (not counting the brother who died shortly after birth), that was quite a while in our family history.

She sent me to a box in her bedroom and asked that I bring it to her in the kitchen. Since her hands were sticky with some

The Other Marconi

morsels of dough and flour from her board, I didn't hesitate to oblige her. When I brought the box out to the kitchen, she told me to open it and to go deep into the stack of photos that were contained inside.

I found a copy of their wedding picture and realized what a handsome couple they were at the time of their marriage. Although my mother's appearance in the photo was not as striking as my father's because of her thin frame, they were indeed an attractive couple. My father was not smiling, but he was strikingly handsome and contained all the pride that a young Italian man could possess. "Do you understand now what I'm saying? The ladies would not leave your father alone. It was not always his fault that he would get into trouble."

I asked her what she meant by 'him getting into trouble.' *Apparently, this conversation occurred before I was privy to the 'hunting cabin' episode.* She told me to ask my father. She continued by asking me if I had ever heard of the old phrase: 'Russian hands and Roman fingers!' I stopped to think what that meant and then...I got the picture. I bolted slightly and responded, "Oh... not Dad?" She quickly replied, "Yes, your Dad." And if I hadn't kept him in check all these years his good looks and confidence in himself would have made trouble for us." "Now," she continued, "go back into the box and find a photo of your father holding his slide trombone." When I located that photo I realized that he looked like a Rock Star of the Victorian period!

As I watched my mother rolling her dough on the board an amusing thought came to mind. My mother asked me why I was smiling and I lied and told her that I was smiling because I realized how handsome my parents were and how they both must have been popular party people. But...I was really smiling with amusement because I recalled the 'Maggie and Jiggs' comic strip and how Maggie was often chasing Jiggs around the house with her rolling pin! Jiggs was so often in 'the dog house.'

During that same conversation, my mother reminded me that there was no shortage of attention for my father where his sisters were concerned. I did understand that statement. There were a few times during my years at home when we did take that long distance drive to Linden, New Jersey where all of my father's family had settled: Roy and his three sisters.

My Aunt Rose and Aunt Mary were especially attentive to my father during those visits; he was their "rock star" and he knew it. My Aunt Nancy lived in a neighboring community, but my Aunts Rose and Mary usually worked together in Aunt Rose Micale's kitchen to prepare for our visit.

My Aunt Rose was pleased to inform us that in order to prepare for our visit she and her sister had begun the preparations of specialty foods a week in advance. I could understand why when she took me to her refrigerator and freezer to proudly show the ravioli, manicotti and other homemade pastas that were awaiting our arrival.

My Uncle Frank had been sent into the city (New York City was less than twenty miles from Linden) to pick up the fresh cannolis and cookies filled with almond paste and other desserts that one usually associates with extravagant Italian weddings. These specialties were all being brought forth because Brother Mike and his family had come to visit!

After that conversation I never questioned my mother's motive for keeping the compliments on his inventive ideas 'left-handed,' rather than being too encouraging. But I decided that I could encourage him when I thought that he had a worthy idea for patent consideration. And so, between his loyal siblings and his children, "Marconi" did not suffer a lack of kudos and attention.

Chapter 37

And the Band Plays On

During the same years of weddings and a new car and continued progress by both Mike, at insurance, and Lucy, with her several business ventures…Mike became more and more engrossed in the radio programs of World News and Operas broadcast by "The Voice of Firestone." I can still recall the theme song from that program, *"If I could tell you how much I love you…"* There were not many things that I had in common with my father, but an interest in opera did become one of them. And my favorite opera became that of Leoncavallo's "Pagliacci."

For an individual who had never attended a live opera, my father knew a great deal about the Italian composers and the various arias which he was able to readily identify with the associated operas. While Italian opera was his primary interest, he did know some of the more famous operas performed by the French and German composers: some of those were works of Berlioz and Wagner.

Perhaps his favorite Italian composer was Verdi. And I recall that when the $64,000 Question was a popular television show, my father was able to quickly answer to that most valuable question asked of the contestant in the sound proof booth. The question pertained to an opera by Verdi and the answer was "Aida." It took my father only a matter of seconds after the question to call out that $64,000 answer.

During this same period of time my father's creative mind continued to come up with new ideas to present to the Office of Patents and Inventions. In fact, it was probably during these chapters of his life that he most gingerly advanced with the notion that one day his creative ideas would be the products enjoyed by the masses.

In 1951 Lucy's "Marconi" was once again called in by his district manager to receive praises for his outstanding production in insurance sales. The gold fab was recalled so that a larger diamond could replace the original smaller one. He was reminded that in five years a larger diamond and one of considerable value would replace this beautiful stone.

There were rumors beginning to circulate regarding the agency adding health insurance to their various programs which were exclusively related to life policies at the time. This news concerned my father greatly because of his limited education and the notion that he would have to enroll in some business courses in order to become licensed for this additional category of insurance.

He had sometimes struggled with the bookkeeping that was required to turn in weekly reports. But he had enjoyed the assistance of my sister, Mary Lou, who was an 'A' student and enjoyed a reputation for being quick in solving mathematical problems. But now she was married and he had no one in the family to lean on. By the end of 1950 all five daughters were married!

Suddenly, the grand house with a wrap-around porch that had been known as "the little White House" had become impractical for the family. Now that family was a family of four: my parents and my brother and me.

A home that had once been envisioned to hold engagement parties and wedding celebrations was now going to be home for busy professional parents and two sons who were only thirteen and eleven. There was certainly not going to be any weddings in the

The Other Marconi

future. The only large gatherings were restricted to an occasional birthday party. *I was the son who relished those gatherings.*

Another move was planned to downsize with the family's decrease in numbers. It was decided that the large white house would be sold and we would move into apartments in a rather handsome Victorian three-story which had been purchased in 1948 as an investment property.

It was a magnificent three-story custom-designed Victorian structure that had been built for two physicians and their wives. The physicians were brother-in-laws who had their family practices and residence in the eighteen room quasi-mansion which boasted a New England Colonial-style porch and slate roof.

The only deficiency of this lovely property was the fact that it was heated by a coal-fired nine section boiler that would now be fired by the strong coal-mining arms of my father. (Previously, it had been the duties of one of the tenants who enjoyed a generous discount in his monthly rent).

I seldom offered to share the burden of firing that monster of a furnace; it was a known fact that neither my brother nor I had inherited the strength and physical stamina that my father had gained as a teenage boy. And so it was seldom that I offered to participate in the daily ritual of firing that huge iron monster during the winter months.

It was on a shelf near the coal bin that my father had kept his diary in a black metal box, covered with an old towel that he used to wipe his hands after shoveling the coal.

I should note that just about the time that I was entering the army (my father now in his early sixties), my parents finally converted the nine section boiler to gas. But my father continued to keep the black box hidden under the old towel. And he continued to visit that box to make entries that were known only to him.

As usual, Mike's involvement was going along at settlement to offer his signature to the closing documents of property purchases or sales. Of course in the 1950's a bank would have never granted a mortgage to a woman without the husband's involvement, but my father never brought that to my mother's attention. He acknowledged that these purchases were all of her doing.

Chapter 38

Retirement

The year was 1954 and Mike was just two years away from that most prestigious diamond being placed in the beautiful gold fab. But he was content that the gold locket held the pictures of his two sons and reminded my mother that it belonged to her. He had wanted her to wear it shortly after he was first awarded it, but she feared that it could attract a thief. Also, she never wore anything around her neck; she was uncomfortable in doing so. Instead she did value a nice pin to go on the upper left side of her dress—when she was wearing a dressy dress.

And so that year Michael Albano, the poor boy from a small town in Reggio Calabria, retired from the Prudential Insurance Company with twenty-eight years of distinguished sales performance.

It's worth noting that just as Lucy's Marconi had not consulted her in the purchase of that 1948 Chevrolet neither did he consult her in his decision to retire. He may have informed her the week before he turned in his books, but there was no discussion about how it may affect family finances.

Mike had learned years ago that when his wife made a decision to do something, his approval or disapproval was like the rhetoric question…why ask? And so he had learned to make decisions void of her consultation. That did not bode well with Lucy in this case, however. He was quick to assure her that he was not retiring from work!

He admitted he lacked confidence in returning to school in order to learn the necessary intricacies of health insurance and subsequently prepare for the required examinations that would lead to licensure.

Shortly after retiring, friends and relatives began asking him what he was going to do now. Was Lucy retiring also? Of course that was a rhetorical question! She had just opened a family-style restaurant in their home and was still managing her apartments, as well as operating a furniture store six days of the week.

Sure enough Mike found employment…and it was right in front of our Front Street residence. New gas lines were being installed throughout the town.

I should inform my readers that at no time had Mike Albano ever lost the strength that he had developed during those earlier years in the coal mines. He would often flex his muscles to show a bulging muscle and he could make it move (one friend called it 'the dancing bicep)! In his earlier days, he would amuse my brother and me as small children by making the muscle jump. For us it was like watching a magic show!

My father truly enjoyed entertaining small children who would visit. He was especially good at making a child stop crying by his amusing antics. And he always was ready to offer a horsey ride to a pouting child. Little boys were especially amused by this entertainment. My father would put a child on his knee and then making a galloping sound he moved his knee to imitate a pony ride.

His decision to work hard labor in his mid-fifties was not very amusing to my mother, however. There were some challenging days ahead shortly after his surprise retirement.

Several of the town's women would stop to admire 'Marconi' operating the jack hammer on the street. They would often approach my mother with complimentary remarks about my father's ability to do such physically demanding work at his age.

The Other Marconi

My mother was not amused by this exhibition of his virility. And such remarks only infuriated her and caused friction between them. Fortunately, the job did not last long and after a few days at the jack hammer the employer apparently viewed the job to be a liability for the company. After two or three years the winds calmed and they found common ground.

Shortly after my graduation from high school my parents decided to visit my oldest sister who had moved from Philadelphia to a small town just outside of Atlantic City. I'm not sure if my brother accompanied them on that trip or chose to remain behind for part of the summer with school friends. But it was my mother's first visit to the infamous Atlantic City.

While there, the wheels of business were spinning in my mother's head. Mike was pleased that his 'Bashful Lucy' liked the shore and could now associate that venue with boardwalk and ocean, rather than the convention that hosted a strip show!

The following summer my mother closed the furniture store… temporarily, placing a sign in the window that read: "will return next season," and although 'next season' sometimes resulted in several seasons she was sure her customers would be ready to welcome her back whenever she returned!

It was rather easy to close down the restaurant because we did not employ individuals outside of the family. My sister Roseann sometimes waited tables and my father was happy to do anything in the kitchen from cooking to dishwashing. *I must admit that I had become quite good at filling pizza shells and making hoagies a/k/a gyro sandwiches.*

My father was happy to help out in the Atlantic City restaurant but the kitchen was small and only accommodated one cook and a dishwasher. He was willing to wait tables, but both of my parents acknowledged that my father no longer had a steady hand for serving meals. My brother waited tables and so my father began considering employment elsewhere. It was perhaps the first year that he entertained the idea of working at the very hotel where they had taken lodging.

The restaurant in Atlantic City lasted two seasons and then my parents decided to take vacation there. Mike had decided that his wife needed the vacation more than he did and…besides the job as desk clerk would pay the rent for a hotel room.

'The Other Marconi,' who by now had given up on his inventions being patented, began working as a night desk clerk at the very hotel to which they had become familiar from the previous two years. During the day both Mike and Lucy enjoyed the bingo games and a short walk on the boardwalk with many periodic rest stops. And after a few hours of sleep in the early evening, he would assume his duties at the hotel desk.

The 'Atlantic Shuttle Bus' lasted from the late 1950's to early 1960's and then Atlantic City became too commercial with the advent of the casinos.

It was the late 1960's when Lucy decided to close her furniture store permanently and Mike, at the age of seventy, was content to finally accept retirement. He also had put aside his earlier ambitions to invent. Retirement for 'Bashful Lucy' and her 'other Marconi' only lasted for a few years, however, as we shall soon learn.

I could sense that my parents were both 'antsy' about staying home all day. It was not a lifestyle that either of them had ever learned to enjoy…especially after the children were all gone and they were true empty nesters.

Chapter 39

Play it Again Sam!

In 1970 my Uncle Roy and Aunt Nervie were celebrating their 50th wedding anniversary. I had visited my cousin Teresa and her husband Al in Linden the year prior to her parents' 50th and they shared the elaborate plans they had in motion for the happy occasion. There would be an orchestra and dinner at a convention center for a large number of guests: the immediate family which now included nieces and nephews and grandchildren and…even some great grandchildren…and close friends of their parents.

So in 1970 many of my family members attended and of course my parents were present. My father wouldn't have missed it for all the world. Here was Roy, age 74 and my father 72 and the two couples were enjoying each other's company after many years which had passed since those early coal mining days in Morrisdale. The men had decades ago retired their flirtatious habits of pinching, but I'm not sure that their wives were ever convinced of that retirement!

Everyone attending was happy to witness seeing these couples and other members of the family reunite under such pleasant and joyful circumstances. And then…as the band stopped playing after a set of old and familiar songs, something happened that to this day chokes me with nostalgic memory. My father walked up to the band and said something to the bandleader. Within a few minutes, my father was handed a slide trombone while the entire room of guests brought their chatter to a whisper. Shortly thereafter, he began playing the theme song from The Voice of Firestone: "If I could tell you how much I love you…."

I had never heard my father play the trombone! I had no idea that he could still play an instrument that he had not played for more than fifty years! To this day I have no idea how he had learned to play that song!

After he played a few chords of the melody, he put the instrument down and walked over to hug his brother. The room was mixed with applause and tears. It was perhaps the most singular emotional event that I had ever witnessed in my family.

It is only now, years later, that I am able to fully understand the love that these two brothers held for each other. If there was ever any doubt that my father was a "romantic" that gesture would have dismissed the doubt.

Chapter 40
Happy Days are here Again

The wedding anniversary of 1970 generated some thoughts and ideas for me. My wheels began spinning and for one solid year leading up to August 22, 1972, not a day went by that I was not in the process of producing and directing an extravaganza for my parents' 50th.

And so on that August day, a Fiftieth Anniversary celebration was planned and delivered without a hitch! I had an extra tuxedo which I loaned to my father and the day began with an informal reception of immediate family at my home in Good Hope Farms. The bride of fifty years was enjoying a short nap before her daughters, three of whom were licensed beauticians, began the hair styling and preparation for her wedding dress (a beautiful golden yellow cocktail gown).

From the house, a large caravan of cars drove to St. Joseph's Catholic Church in Mechanicsburg where three priests—all friends of the family concelebrated a mass with the renewal of vows. From there we went to the Carlisle Country Club where a reception was followed by a sit-down dinner for more than a hundred guests with a strolling violinist who first serenaded my parents and then went from table to table playing requests of the dinner guests. The dinner was followed by an orchestra that played for the dancing guests into the night.

One would think that perhaps that would complete a chapter into the life of 'The Other Marconi' and his 'Bashful Lucy,' but it was only the beginning of a new chapter!

Shortly after the anniversary celebration I got a call from my parents. They had decided to go back into business; my mother was in the process of assembling an entirely new inventory of furniture—both new and used.

Apparently the excitement of the anniversary had brought new energy into them and this time my father was going to participate in the store. He assured me that in no way would he let his bride operate a business without being by her side.

After working the coal mines, making picture frames, selling insurance, operating a jack hammer, and working the night shift at an Atlantic City hotel, Mike a/k/a Marconi was finally going to be a partner in his wife's furniture store!

For the next four or five years Mike would go out to warm up the car while his bride of fifty plus years would fiddle around inside making sure that she had all that she needed to have a successful day at her store.

My father proudly wore the diamond ring that I had given him as an anniversary gift. My mother was not comfortable wearing her diamond in the store where it may send a wrong signal to lower-income buyers. But my father had no compunction about wearing his one carat diamond ring. He was proud to wear the gift that marked their fifty years of marriage.

Chapter 41

The Winter of Their Lives

It was only a few years after the 50th wedding anniversary that my mother had to make a major change in her life. At first, only my father was aware of the necessary change and secret. She kept a wheelchair in the back of her store, hidden from the public. But shortly after arriving at the store, she would surrender to that wheelchair and remain seated behind her desk. When customers came into the store she would invite them to look around and then Mike would accompany them to the desk with their purchases. The wheelchair was not easily revealed.

This little secret was kept from the family for a short while longer than from the general public. But eventually we discovered the necessary change and finally my mother was bound to her wheelchair. Among other complications, severe arthritis had taken a toll on her ability to walk.

Mike's turn of events could not be concealed as easily as my mother's ability to hide behind her desk, however. The tremors in both hands began to be noticeable just about the time he was celebrating his eightieth birthday.

At first the shaking could be controlled by resting his hands on his lap. Being a very strong-willed woman, my mother refused to allow the disease, known as Parkinson's, to interfere with Mike's ability to function in a normal manner. But just as Mike had assisted his Bashful Lucy in concealing her secret, now when the couple were alone she would assist him with his eating so that he did not feel embarrassed at the risk of shaking the food off of his spoon. Each one of these individuals were intent on preserving the dignity of the other.

My fondest memory of my parents was the lasting picture that I recorded in my mind of driving off after a short visit and watching my parents through that large glass showroom window at the entrance of their store with this loving couple, caring for each other and preserving whatever years remained in the beautiful life of Bashful Lucy and her very own Marconi.

Reflections

I never went fishing with my father because he did not grow up knowing the pleasures of the outdoors. He wouldn't have been able to teach me how to throw out a line. And I never learned to hunt… probably for two reasons: my mother never allowed firearms in our home and…I doubt if my father could have pulled the trigger on an innocent and helpless animal. The great outdoors was just not an area of interest for my father and…as it turned out, neither for me. Camping and the perks that go with it were never at the forefront of my interests.

My father did enjoy being a television spectator of boxing, but that sport never transferred to my interests. I could not find the logic in one human being trying to intentionally injure another—unless in the operation of war. But his deep interest in foreign languages—communicating with his fellowmen in their native tongue and his interest in world affairs and politics and passion for Italian Opera absolutely did succeed in leaving a lifetime imprint on me.

It was during the late 60's and early 70's that I frequented the Metropolitan Opera. Of course mobile phones had not yet made their debut into our society, so it was the pay phone in the lobby of the Met where I would ring up my father during intermission and share with him the first act of the performance. It was always an opera with which he had become extremely familiar: Verdi's "Aida," or "Nabucco" or Leoncavallo's "Pagliacci" or one of Puccini's many great works.

I had only recalled one aria from my youth, *Vesti la Giubba* from "Pagliacci," but quickly became as familiar with the arias from many others that had all become among my favorites. So the evenings at home when my father had his ear glued to the radio for World News or the Firestone Theatre, I became exposed to those areas of interest that allowed me to inherit the passion for opera and the intense concern for World Affairs and an interest that has led me to become a 'political junkie.'

It is only natural that when I hear the aria from "Aida" I look back on a particular evening when we sat, as a family, around the black and white TV watching the "Sixty-Four Thousand Dollar Question" and that same evening when my father quickly answered the question that would have resulted in the contestant winning that all-important prize of $64,000! Yes, the answer was "Aida," but as I recall the contestant who was isolated in that sound-proof booth had not known Italian operas as my father did. I think that evening gave us reason to respect his love and knowledge of opera.

And perhaps it was those occasional (twice each year) times when my father would invite my brother and me to ride along with him for a day of collecting the insurance premiums from the homes of his foreign-born clients that brought about my own fascination for learning foreign languages. I can still hear him greeting the woman who answered the door in her native tongue—sometimes in Swedish, or German or Russian. He never purported to be fluent, but his limited knowledge of their native tongue always brought a smile upon their face as they responded to his kind inquiry of their family.

And how could I forget how clever he was in allowing himself to be conned by my youngest sisters when we were driving to visit my grandmother in Walston. He knew that it was not a coincidence that they had to use the restroom when we were approaching the Keystone Ice Cream factory as we passed through Clearfield. It was true that there were restrooms in the area of the ice cream parlor, but of course once inside there was no question as to purchasing large cones of ice cream. He would smile as he pretended that he did not associate the request for ice cream cones with that sudden urge to use the restroom.

Author's note

More could be written about this remarkable gentleman, who truly exemplified the meaning of the word "gentleman" throughout his life without ever having a formal education that is so often associated with that title. But I believe that this story will allow the reader to know enough about the man who began his life in one of the poorest villages of southern Italy and with pride and humility went on to live a life that won him the respect and affection of all with whom he came in contact…a man who went into the coal mines of Pennsylvania until he was discovered to be worthy of wearing a three-piece suit and offering life insurance to those other miners who would spend most of their lives in those deep holes. To those families he was forever a hero who played a part, not only in their financial survival, but in insuring their families' futures for formal education through those policies.

Mike Albano was a man who never allowed his love of family to be distracted by the trappings of financial success or title. And he was never ashamed to admit that he prayed for his parents every day…long after their passing. His faith was displayed by his actions, rather than his words.

Dedication

I dedicate this story to the memory of my parents, Mike and Lucy (né Michele and Maria Lucia) Albano. For parents who were born of poor Italian beginnings and who 'pulled themselves up by their bootstraps' to become the successful parents, neighbors, respected citizens of their community, entrepreneurs, and loving grandparents, they were truly under-appreciated, under-acknowledged, but much loved by their children and grandchildren. It's purely by accident, and not planning, that I chose the titles for their books that was the same titles that each had bestowed on the other: **Bashful Lucy and The Other Marconi.**

Acknowledgment

I would like to give a special thanks to Marie Tomasi for her unwavering support and dedication to helping me with each of my writing projects to insure that each word and each line of each paragraph is exactly as I have intended it to appear and that her occasional editing ideas and improvements have allowed me to become a better writer.